PRACTICAL
FENG SHUI

Symbols of Good Fortune

LILLIAN TOO'S

PRACTICAL
FENG SHUI

Symbols of Good Fortune

For Jennifer, my sweetheart of a daughter … with love

First published in Great Britain in 2000 by
ELEMENT BOOKS LIMITED
Shaftesbury, Dorset SP7 8BP

Published in the USA in 2000 by ELEMENT BOOKS INC.
160 North Washington Street,
Boston MA 02114

Published in Australia in 2000 by
ELEMENT BOOKS LIMITED
and distributed by
Penguin Australia Ltd
487 Maroondah Highway,
Ringwood, Victoria 3134

Designed and created for Element Books with
The Bridgewater Book Company Ltd

ELEMENT BOOKS LIMITED
Editorial Director Sue Hook
Project Editor Kate Adams
Text Editor Emma Callery
Production Director Clare Armstrong

THE BRIDGEWATER BOOK COMPANY
Art Director Terry Jeavons
Designer Alistair Plumb
Editorial Director Fiona Biggs
Project Editor Mark Truman
Photography Mike Hemsley, Walter Gardiner Photography
Illustrations Lorraine Harrison, Sarah Young, Rhian Nest James
Three-dimensional models Mark Jamieson
Picture research Liz Eddison

Printed and bound in the UK by
Butler and Tanner Ltd

ISBN 1 86204 795 2

The publishers wish to thank the following
for the use of properties:
Bright Ideas, Spellbound and Spirit,
and Elizabeth Simmonds Private Collection in Lewes;
Adaptatrap, Evolution, C&H Fabrics,
and Goy Chinese Medicine Centre in Brighton.

The publishers wish to thank the following for the use of pictures:

AKG 8, 66L, 93B; **The Bridgeman Art Library** 9 (British Library, London, UK), 23 (Christie's Images), 57B (British Library, London, UK),
69 (Osterreichische Galerie, Vienna), 81T (Christie's Images), 123 (Oriental Museum, Durham University);
Goh Seng Chong 10, 11, 31, 37R, 39, 44T, 44B, 45, 47, 55, 59B, 71BL, 71BR, 70B, 79, 94, 95, 99, 106, 107B, 120;
Tony Stone 16B (Davies & Starr), 19 (David C. Tomlinson), 57T (David Muench), 81B (Dianne Flumara), 92 (Art Wolfe),
107T (Gavin Hellier), 114 (Rex Butcher); **The Image Bank** (Michael Melford), 22TL (Pete Turner), 22TR (Anselm Spring), 22C (Malcolm Piers),
22BR (Nino Mascardi), 62B (Kevin Rose), 71T (Bob Elsdale); **The Stock Market** 21;
Bruce Coleman 32T, 35B, 36BR, 56T, 56B, 66R, 89, 93T; **Corbis** 53, 76; **Liz Eddison** 109

CONTENTS

INTRODUCTION

Here are all the symbols of good fortune you can use to jazz up your love life, help you live a healthy life to a ripe old age, enhance your career luck, and make you have a happier working life. They will help you to attain recognition and the respect of your peers and colleagues, ensure excellent descendants' luck for you, enable you to nurture a happy and harmonious family, and even help you get seriously rich. Symbols of good fortune manifest the positive aspects of Chi energies within your living space, and in the following pages you will discover how you can use them to decorate and embellish the energies in your home and office.

The Power of Symbols in Feng Shui

All Chinese characters and words are essentially pictures that communicate their meanings through the visual. Chinese words are more graphic than phonetic, reflecting the Chinese penchant for viewing most objects as containing hidden meanings that are symbolic of either good luck or misfortune. Thus the Chinese see a great many objects as conveyors of symbolic good or bad luck, and they view events as signs – portents of good or bad tidings.

Pictures contain more meaning than is at first evident. And these meanings can be obvious or hidden. Usually, however, symbolic meanings are seldom grasped at first glance – except by those who have learned to look beyond the obvious.

Hidden meanings associated with objects and events often have greater potency than ordinary language can describe. The symbolism of Chinese beliefs is rich with nuances and contains multiple shades of meanings. Thus, for example, in a Chinese landscape painting there are meanings in the way clouds, trees, mountains, rocks, streams, grass, and the characters have been drawn. To the untrained eye, the painting shows a scenic view, nothing more. But to the trained eye, expert in the hidden meanings of Feng Shui symbols, the way the clouds are shaped, the selection of trees, the positioning of the water, rocks, and grass, and finally the shape and orientation of mountains in the painting can indicate messages of good will.

There may either be prosperity meanings or hidden poison arrows inadvertently placed so that the painting becomes an inauspicious purveyor of killing breath. Chinese artists of the old days were thus knowledgeable about the more popular good fortune symbols. This enhanced the marketability of their works and increased their commissioned business.

THE ORIGINS OF GOOD FORTUNE SYMBOLS

The origins of good fortune symbols are usually legends and myths that have survived the centuries by word of mouth. Rarely are these symbols used in an esoteric or religious sense. Instead, they are regarded as emblems that complement the good Feng Shui of a home, and they are chosen to express goodwill and friendship in a social sense.

The function of symbols is to bring good luck to households and express good wishes to friends during festive and other happy occasions. Symbols thus play a significant role in the giving of gifts. As in the Western tradition of bringing flowers to a friend or relative for birthdays, anniversaries, and other celebratory occasions, so the Chinese bring a vase, a painted dish, or an embroidered purse – each decorated with symbols that express the kind of good fortune appropriate to the occasion.

Thus peaches and cranes are always suitable for birthdays since these express the wish for long life, implicit in which is good health. The double happiness sign or a pair of mandarin ducks are great as a wedding present; a peony is excellent for the coming of age of a young daughter; and the jade scepter of authority is a very suitable graduation gift, since it denotes good wishes for a bright career; and so it goes on. There are symbols to suit almost every *hei see*, or happy occasion.

Naturally, such auspicious gifts would be most inappropriate for those wishing to express condolences at the loss of a member of the family. For such sad Yin occasions, symbolism is usually kept to a minimum.

Modern recipients of this kind of carefully thought-out gift should inspect and study the decorative symbols carefully to identify the exact good wishes being conveyed. Usually, the accompanying calligraphy on paintings offers additional clues to the meaning of the symbolism.

CRANES HAVE LONG BEEN
ASSOCIATED WITH LONGEVITY.
MANY PICTURES FEATURE THESE
ELEGANT BIRDS.

SELECTING THE SYMBOLS

When selecting the symbols for this book, I have been influenced by their relevance and practicality in this modern age. There are thousands of symbols in the Chinese pantheon, but I have chosen only those deemed to represent good fortune. I have also allowed myself a certain amount of leeway, picking only the symbols I like and those that I can recommend with genuine conviction. I have either used them with a certain amount of success or I have seen them displayed in the homes of wealthy and successful people. I have also chosen those that practitioners of Feng Shui whom I trust and respect have personally recommended to me.

Use this book as a reference guide to ascertain the meanings of Chinese decorative symbols. Select the symbols that appeal to you and take your time inviting them into your home. Do not rush into filling your home with all the suggestions contained in these pages. It is better to go slowly. Shop with care. In your enthusiasm do not overpay for a decorative object just because it has a motif or symbol you want, nor should you purchase a vase with flowers when you do not like the shape of the vase. Likewise, don't display a traditional dragon if you feel it will clash with the decor of your home. In using symbols of good fortune, there is always room for good taste and good design. Let your creativity flow and remember that symbols need not be traditional, antique, or Chinese in origin to work.

Categories of Good Fortune Symbols

The categories of good fortune symbols reflect humans as the cardinal beings around which animals, plants, and artifacts have meaning. Then there is the unity of heaven and earth and the deities that symbolize wealth. Even natural phenomena – clouds, rain, dew, thunder – take on deep symbolic meanings.

The most prevalent symbols of good fortune used to enhance Feng Shui are the celestial creatures of the heavenly realm. Of these, the dragon, the phoenix, and the unicorn are said to be legendary and mythical. No one knows for sure if these creatures ever existed in the past but they certainly do not exist today. The celestial dragon is regarded as the ultimate good luck symbol, and his image is generally regarded as auspicious. When placed in the south, all feathered creatures symbolize the Chi of the celestial phoenix (*see* page 40). There are other legendary creatures whose images are likewise said to bring about happy events, and although, with the exception of the tortoise, they no longer exist, they continue to be regarded with favor.

Then there are the animals of the earthly realm. In Feng Shui, these animals are viewed as symbols of protection. Tigers, horses, and elephants, each has specific connotations of good luck. Of this category, the fu dogs are the best known – made famous by the picture of the fu dogs in the Forbidden Palace complex of Beijing.

There are also good fortune plants, auspicious fruits, and special flowers that symbolize love, purity,

AMONG THE PANTHEON OF CHINESE ANIMALS, THE CELESTIAL DRAGON IS REGARDED AS THE MOST IMPORTANT.

and beauty. Images of these and other symbols of good fortune magnify the effects of correct Feng Shui orientations and in many instances also speed up the positive impact of Feng Shui.

THE CELESTIAL CREATURES

The celestial creatures of the Feng Shui compass highlight the preliminary set of symbols used in Feng Shui. Thus the dragon, tiger, phoenix, and tortoise make up the first set of creatures that can be energized to bring great good fortune to the home. These four are the most important of the symbols and are covered in greater detail on pages 38, 40, 59, and 92.

In many of the old classical texts on Feng Shui the environment that surrounds a home is lyrically described in terms of the dragon and tiger presence to the left and right of the house respectively. These creatures are often interpreted to mean hills, mountains, and elevated land. It is for this reason that undulating land is always considered to be more auspicious than completely flat land.

Urban dwellers who reside in places where the land is flat and there is no presence of dragons can, however, simulate the green dragon by displaying its vibrant image on the east wall of the living room. This is believed successfully to create the cosmic Chi of the dragon inside the home. A painting of a dragon need not be large for it to bring good fortune. Small paintings or even a postcard-size print of a Chinese dragon correctly placed along the east wall of your living room is sufficient to energize the precious breath of the dragon. The use of symbolism in Feng Shui thus starts with the dragon image.

As for the tiger, it is best not to put an image of the tiger inside the house because it can turn its great ferocity against the place in which it dwells. However, tigers placed outside the home next to the main door take on protective energies for the residents. It

THE DRAGON AND PHOENIX MOTIF EXPRESSES MARITAL BLISS.

is, however, extremely beneficial to simulate both the phoenix and the tortoise (or turtle) inside the home. These two creatures are potent and significant good-fortune energizers. Place the phoenix in the south. In Feng Shui terms this means either the south of the living room or the south of the home itself or even the south of the land plot. The phoenix can be placed inside the home or outside in the yard. Activating the phoenix brings many different types of luck, the most important of which is the luck of money-making opportunities.

The tortoise is one of the most auspicious creatures to have in the home or around the garden. Place the tortoise in the north. Once again, in Feng Shui terms this means either the north of the living room, of the home, or of the yard. Find out where north is in your home by using any Western compass.

THE TWELVE ANIMALS OF THE CHINESE ZODIAC

In addition to the four celestial creatures another set of animals also features prominently in Feng Shui practice. These are the 12 animals of the Chinese zodiac – the rat, ox, tiger, rabbit, dragon, snake, horse, sheep, monkey, dog, rooster, and pig. Each of these animals has a corresponding direction that occupies 30 degrees of the compass, providing clues for positioning images of these animals to magnify their energy. The table on page 12 summarizes the 12 animals of the zodiac and their corresponding directions.

Using the 100-year lunar calendar (*see* pages 12–13), find out the animal sign that rules your own birth chart. You can then determine from the table which sector of your home corresponds to your ruling "animal." Now you can place an image of that animal in the sector of your living room that corresponds to that direction.

For example, if you were born in May 1957 (the year of the rooster), the corresponding number would be 10 in the chart, which represents the direction west. So placing, say, a ceramic rooster in the west would energize the earthly branch of your Four Pillars chart. And if you were born in the year of the tiger, then it would be beneficial to place an image of a tiger in the east-northeast sector of your living room (which corresponds to direction 3 in the chart). This is a simplified technique of applying symbolic Feng Shui based on the Four Pillars method. For more information on how to use the 12 animals to enhance your Feng Shui *see* pages 124–139.

DETERMINING YOUR ANIMAL SIGN

WESTERN CALENDAR DATES	ANIMAL SIGN
18 Feb 1912 – 5 Feb 1913	Rat
6 Feb 1913 – 25 Jan 1914	Ox
26 Jan 1914 – 13 Feb 1915	Tiger
14 Feb 1915 – 2 Feb 1916	Rabbit
3 Feb 1916 – 22 Jan 1917	Dragon
23 Jan 1917 – 10 Feb 1918	Snake
11 Feb 1918 – 31 Jan 1919	Horse
1 Feb 1919 – 19 Feb 1920	Sheep
20 Feb 1920 – 7 Feb 1921	Monkey
8 Feb 1921 – 27 Jan 1922	Rooster
28 Jan 1922 – 15 Feb 1923	Dog
16 Feb 1923 – 4 Feb 1924	Boar

START OF 60-YEAR CYCLE

5 Feb 1924 – 23 Jan 1925	Rat
24 Jan 1925 – 12 Feb 1926	Ox
13 Feb 1926 – 1 Feb 1927	Tiger
2 Feb 1927 – 22 Jan 1928	Rabbit
23 Jan 1928 – 9 Feb 1929	Dragon
10 Feb 1929 – 29 Jan 1930	Snake
30 Jan 1930 – 16 Feb 1931	Horse
17 Feb 1931 – 5 Feb 1932	Sheep
6 Feb 1932 – 25 Jan 1933	Monkey
26 Jan 1933 – 13 Feb 1934	Rooster
14 Feb 1934 – 3 Feb 1935	Dog
4 Feb 1935 – 23 Jan 1936	Boar
24 Jan 1936 – 10 Feb 1937	Rat
11 Feb 1937 – 30 Jan 1938	Ox
31 Jan 1938 – 18 Feb 1939	Tiger
19 Feb 1939 – 7 Feb 1940	Rabbit
8 Feb 1940 – 26 Jan 1941	Dragon
27 Jan 1941 – 14 Feb 1942	Snake
15 Feb 1942 – 4 Feb 1943	Horse
5 Feb 1943 – 24 Jan 1944	Sheep

THE HOUSE DIRECTIONS OF THE TWELVE ANIMALS

NUMBER	ANIMAL	DIRECTION
1	Rat	North
2	Ox	North-northeast
3	Tiger	East-northeast
4	Rabbit	East
5	Dragon	East-southeast
6	Snake	South-southeast
7	Horse	South
8	Sheep	South-southwest
9	Monkey	West-southwest
10	Rooster	West
11	Dog	West-northwest
12	Boar	North-northwest

DETERMINING YOUR ANIMAL SIGN

WESTERN CALENDAR DATES	ANIMAL SIGN
25 Jan 1944 – 12 Feb 1945	Monkey
13 Feb 1945 – 1 Feb 1946	Rooster
2 Feb 1946 – 21 Jan 1947	Dog
22 Jan 1947 – 9 Feb 1948	Boar
10 Feb 1948 – 28 Jan 1949	Rat
29 Jan 1949 – 16 Feb 1950	Ox
17 Feb 1950 – 5 Feb 1951	Tiger
6 Feb 1951 – 26 Jan 1952	Rabbit
27 Jan 1952 – 13 Feb 1953	Dragon
14 Feb 1953 – 2 Feb 1954	Snake
3 Feb 1954 – 23 Jan 1955	Horse
24 Jan 1955 – 11 Feb 1956	Sheep
12 Feb 1956 – 30 Jan 1957	Monkey
31 Jan 1957 – 17 Feb 1958	Rooster
18 Feb 1958 – 7 Feb 1959	Dog
8 Feb 1959 – 27 Jan 1960	Boar
28 Jan 1960 – 14 Feb 1961	Rat
15 Feb 1961 – 4 Feb 1962	Ox
5 Feb 1962 – 24 Jan 1963	Tiger
25 Jan 1963 – 12 Feb 1964	Rabbit
13 Feb 1964 – 1 Feb 1965	Dragon
2 Feb 1965 – 20 Jan 1966	Snake
21 Jan 1966 – 8 Feb 1967	Horse
9 Feb 1967 – 29 Jan 1968	Sheep
30 Jan 1968 – 16 Feb 1969	Monkey
17 Feb 1969 – 5 Feb 1970	Rooster
6 Feb 1970 – 26 Jan 1971	Dog
27 Jan 1971 – 14 Feb 1972	Boar
15 Feb 1972 – 2 Feb 1973	Rat
3 Feb 1973 – 22 Jan 1974	Ox
23 Jan 1974 – 10 Feb 1975	Tiger
11 Feb 1975 – 30 Jan 1976	Rabbit
31 Jan 1976 – 17 Feb 1977	Dragon
18 Feb 1977 – 6 Feb 1978	Snake
7 Feb 1978 – 27 Jan 1979	Horse
28 Jan 1979 – 15 Feb 1980	Sheep

DETERMINING YOUR ANIMAL SIGN

WESTERN CALENDAR DATES	ANIMAL SIGN
16 Feb 1980 – 4 Feb 1981	Monkey
5 Feb 1981 – 24 Jan 1982	Rooster
25 Jan 1982 – 12 Feb 1983	Dog
13 Feb 1983 – 1 Feb 1984	Boar
2 Feb 1984 – 19 Feb 1985	Rat
20 Feb 1985 – 8 Feb 1986	Ox
9 Feb 1986 – 28 Jan 1987	Tiger
29 Jan 1987 – 16 Feb 1988	Rabbit
17 Feb 1988 – 5 Feb 1989	Dragon
6 Feb 1989 – 26 Jan 1990	Snake
27 Jan 1990 – 14 Feb 1991	Horse
15 Feb 1991 – 3 Feb 1992	Sheep
4 Feb 1992 – 22 Jan 1993	Monkey
23 Jan 1993 – 9 Feb 1994	Rooster
10 Feb 1994 – 30 Jan 1995	Dog
31 Jan 1995 – 18 Feb 1996	Boar
19 Feb 1996 – 6 Feb 1997	Rat
7 Feb 1997 – 27 Jan 1998	Ox
28 Jan 1998 – 15 Feb 1999	Tiger
16 Feb 1999 – 4 Feb 2000	Rabbit
5 Feb 2000 – 23 Jan 2001	Dragon
24 Jan 2001 – 11 Feb 2002	Snake
12 Feb 2002 – 31 Jan 2003	Horse
1 Feb 2003 – 21 Jan 2004	Sheep
22 Jan 2004 – 8 Feb 2005	Monkey
9 Feb 2005 – 28 Jan 2006	Rooster
29 Jan 2006 – 17 Feb 2007	Dog
18 Feb 2007 – 6 Feb 2008	Boar

Good Fortune Symbol Themes

I n addition to the main categories of symbols, there are a number of themes based on the traditional Chinese aspirations that bring happiness – to live a long and healthy life, to attain high social rank and recognition, to have wealth and prosperity, to have successful children, and especially to have sons to carry on the family name.

SYMBOLS OF WEALTH

These symbols are very popular and are described fully on pages 26–47. There are many different categories of wealth symbols – some of which are more potent than others. Perhaps the easiest of the wealth symbols to use are the different kinds of money, coins, and ingots.

Old Chinese coins are extremely popular and also extremely potent in calling upon the luck of both heaven and earth. The square holes in the center of the round coins symbolize the fusion of heaven and earth, bringing prosperity Chi, which is believed to activate and energize prosperity luck.

SYMBOLS OF LONGEVITY

There are symbols that are said to represent all eight of the basic aspirations and in many cases the types of luck overlap. Of the eight symbols, the most popular and widely used are the symbols of longevity, of which there are many (see pages 48–59).

The most significant of these symbols is the God of Longevity, named Sau. His image is featured in many Chinese households that have a prominent patriarch since long life for the patriarch is considered to be of paramount importance.

USE OLD CHINESE COINS TO ATTRACT PROSPERITY TO THE WHOLE HOUSEHOLD.

SYMBOLS OF ROMANCE

This category has many emblems that signify the happiness of love and marriage. These can be used to enhance the luck of love (see pages 60–71).

UNDERSTANDING THE SYMBOLISM

All oriental paintings are meant to be appreciated not simply as works of art. They must be viewed as conveying symbolic meanings. They have characteristic themes such as longevity, prosperity, happiness, and so forth, and these meanings are suggested by images.

Chinese paintings are almost always painted with auspicious themes so that they mean more than simply the images drawn. These images can be plants, trees, animals, flowers, mountains, deities, or humans. There is virtually nothing in the whole of nature, organic or inorganic, no creature, no posture, no color that the Chinese painter does not view as being imbued with symbolic meaning. The skill of the artist lies not just in the way images are painted but also in the way images are combined. Those artists possessing calligraphic talents would also ensure that both image and script would resonate with propitious meanings. Excellent calligraphy – the beautiful rendition of good fortune words – was in itself considered an object of good fortune.

In this way, the form and content of paintings convey hidden nuances of prosperity messages, so prized paintings were valued not merely as works of art. They were deemed superior because of hidden symbolism, and their value would increase tenfold. Such paintings were regarded as purveyors of the good fortune Sheng Chi and were hung in prominent places in the homes of powerful mandarins or warlords.

PLAYING WITH MEANINGS

Clues as to the hidden meanings of images are often provided by puns and other plays on words. Thus a picture of a fish is an expression of abundance because the word for fish – *yu* – means abundance. So when you offer fish to someone you are wishing that person an abundance of wealth. If you keep goldfish it means you are creating the symbolism of an abundance of gold.

To understand symbolism in Feng Shui, it is vital to appreciate the importance of phonetic sounds in the identification of good fortune symbols. The example of fish is only one of many. The interplay of phonetics and puns explains why certain creatures and plants are regarded as objects of good fortune.

For example, the red bat is considered auspicious. According to Chinese belief, the image of the red bat is regarded very favorably since the sound of the word for bat also means great wealth. It is believed that when bats fly to your house to nest they bring good fortune and protection. You should never chase them away. Puns also explain why the number eight is regarded favorably by the Chinese and why the number four is so universally disliked. This is because *eight* sounds like "to grow" while *four* sounds like "to die."

THE VALUE OF COLOR

Bright red or vermilion is the color that brings good fortune. Gifts that are wrapped in red symbolize the giving of premium Yang energy. Red is also worn and used to decorate symbols during marriages, births, and birthday celebrations.

The color red is considered to be especially auspicious, and is widely used during the celebration of weddings and birthdays. Indeed, the traditional Chinese bride is always dressed in red.

Red is also the dominant color during the lunar New Year celebrations. For instance, to ensure a good year, the women of the family are expected to wear a new dress made of red materials. The matriarch distributes gifts of money contained in red packages that have auspicious designs. Red lanterns are lit and hung in front of the main door throughout the 15 days of the New Year, and all fruits and sweetmeats are served on a bed of bright red paper.

THE COLOR RED IS MOST AUSPICIOUS – WRAP BIRTHDAY AND WEDDING PRESENTS WITH RED PAPER AND TIE WITH A GOLD RIBBON TO SIGNIFY PROSPERITY.

Red is not the only good fortune color. Yellow and purple are also auspicious to wear and to use around the home. Yellow has long been considered an Imperial color associated with the emperors, while purple is so lucky that it is regarded by many Feng Shui masters as being even more auspicious than red.

Symbols as Feng Shui Energizers

Chinese symbolism has its origins in legends that go as far back in time as the *I Ching*. Like Feng Shui, symbolism has undergone many variations of form, content, and interpretation. To make good use of these symbols as a supplement to Feng Shui, the principles of Yin and Yang and the five elements must always be taken into account. The effect of symbolism can then be further enhanced by the presence of at least one of the three auspicious hexagrams – chien, kun, and sheng. In this way, the Feng Shui of any space is usually considerably improved.

A great deal of symbolic meaning comes from the Chinese fondness for playing on the sounds of words, on the mythology of Taoism, on the influences of Buddhism, and on the tenets of Confucianism. These combine into a national potpourri of meanings that give symbolism a rich tapestry upon which to paint broad-based manifestations of various types of good fortune. There are variations in the subtle shades of meanings and even the same legend frequently has different versions in different geographical localities.

But overriding all these localized differences is a pervasive acceptance of the good fortune icons as vanguards of happiness, wealth, and long life. Thus all Chinese accept that the dragon is the premier symbol of good fortune, that the phoenix is the harbinger of opportunities, and that the peony is the king of flowers, full of the promise of young love and happiness. These and other well-known, popular symbols are only the tip of the iceberg, however. The list of auspicious symbols is a long one. But simply knowing the meanings of

A PEONY DISPLAYED IN THE HOME ATTRACTS LOVE AND HAPPINESS, ESPECIALLY FOR UNMARRIED WOMEN.

symbols does not do much to energize the Feng Shui of a room or home. Good fortune symbols should be correctly placed in the home or office for them to fulfill the great promise of their meanings.

To do this correctly it is necessary to understand their derivations and the basis on which they are regarded as good fortune symbols. It is also important to understand their Yin or Yang aspects, and the element family they belong to. There is no simple cookbook approach with recipes of good fortune accompanying the symbols.

Symbols can be simple and easy to use or they can possess a plethora of Feng Shui possibilities. Some symbols can bring good fortune wherever they are placed, others require careful diagnosis of their elements and of their Yin or Yang nature before deciding their most auspicious spot. There is also the balance, compatibility, and harmony of the intangible Chi forces to take account of. Furthermore, the questions of size, of the colors, and of the material from which they are made all need to be taken into account.

THE YIN AND YANG OF SYMBOLS

Feng Shui is based on the correct balance of these two primordial forces, and the use of symbols must always take account of this. In the houses of the living, Yang energies are always more meaningful than Yin energies, but the two forces act in consonance, and objects that have a strong symbolic meaning must not upset this balance.

The Yin Yang symbol eloquently describes the balance of these two opposing primordial forces, as can be seen in the simple representation illustrated below. Yin is black and Yang is white. Yin is dark and Yang is bright. All the other attributes of these two forces are likewise opposite to each other in this fashion (*see* pages 23–24 for more information on Yin and Yang). Yet for good Feng Shui energy to be created in any space, working or living, both of these forces (their intrinsic Chi) must not only be present, but they should also be in balance.

This does not mean there needs to be equal doses of each type of Chi energy. What it does mean, is that for abodes of the living, what we call Yang houses, there should be a lot more Yang energy to sustain the energy associated with the living. But there should not be so much Yang energy that Yin disappears completely. In the same way for Yin abodes or the houses of the dead – grave sites and burial grounds – there should be a lot more of Yin than Yang but never to the extent that Yang disappears completely. The principle, therefore, is never to have an excess of either Yang or Yin. When there appears to be an imbalance, you can use symbols to

RAISED LANDFORMS SUCH AS MOUNTAINS ARE YANG, BUT A RANGE OF RIDGED LANDFORMS IS YIN. BOTH ARE NEEDED FOR BALANCE.

correct it. Look again and you will see that in the Yin sector there is a bit of Yang and in the Yang sector there is a bit of Yin.

Symbols of Yin and Yang are categorized according to their attributes, and symbolic Feng Shui requires you to differentiate clearly between Yang objects and Yin objects. Develop an instinctive ability to spot if an object is Yin or Yang before purchasing or displaying it.

But how does the amateur practitioner know which object is Yin and which object is Yang? Moreover, how can the correct balance be obtained? The standard list of Yin and Yang objects is straightforward enough. Thus the sun, noise, white, red, yellow, odd numbers, male, light, heaven, fire, heat, positive forces, and all matter with life represent the Yang force. The moon, silence, black, darkness, female, stillness, even numbers, earth, water, cold, negative forces, ice, and death represent the Yin force.

In Feng Shui orientations it becomes more complex. Raised landforms (mountains) are Yang but a range of ridged landforms is said to be Yin. Valleys and rivers are said to be Yin but they are also said to possess Yang qualities when people settle in the valley and a town is built – Yin and Yang are constantly changing forces. This principle must be applied to the Feng Shui around the home. A useful guideline is to have structures, designs, and objects that seem to be opposite in attributes. Thus land levels should be both flat and raised. There should be light and water, and a profusion of colors. There should be sunlight and shade, and there should also be moonlight.

THE MOON AND YIN ENERGY

In the practice of Feng Shui both Yin and Yang energies must balance at an optimum level to create

A FULL MOON REPRESENTS AN ABUNDANCE OF PURE YIN ENERGY.

good vibrations for the home. In the houses of the living, Yang energies are most precious and vital, but never to the extent that Yin energy becomes absent. Also bedrooms and other rooms meant for rest and relaxation benefit from fresh Yin energy. This is the kind of Yin energy that is good, rather than the stale kind associated with the dead and dying. Thus while we do not want the Yin energy generated by dying plants, for instance, we would welcome the pure Yin energies of a full moon.

THE SUN AND YANG ENERGY

An easy way to capture Yang energy is to ensure the inside of the home gets an occasional bath of sunshine – the sun is the most potent symbol and source of Yang energy. It purifies and energizes at the same time. Homes that receive insufficient sunshine are said to be excessively Yin – a state that spells a surfeit of inauspicious energy. This situation may be caused by overgrown trees or adjacent buildings blocking out the sunlight. Trees that surround any home should be trimmed regularly so precious sunlight shines through.

There are several methods of harnessing the sun's precious Yang energy. Choose one or more of the following to enhance your overall Feng Shui:

- Use Yang energized water to supplement all the water used for watering plants, for filling ponds and aquariums, and for adding to vases for flowers. Place a pail of water out in the sun and let the water stand in direct sunlight for at least three hours. The best sunshine is morning sunshine. Remember that sun energized water is full of life.
- Hang a faceted lead crystal in a window to catch the direct sunlight shining along any wall. The crystal will break up the sunlight and create lots of beautiful rainbows in your home. This will bathe your home with precious Yang energy that creates harmony and a feeling of optimism. I hang these small crystals on many of my windows and thus have rainbows almost daily.
- You can refresh sunshine energies in your home on a regular basis by throwing open all the doors and windows and opening all the drapes and blinds so that sunlight pours in. This cleanses all stagnant and stale Yin energies that may have gathered and accumulated. I recommend you do this once a month.

YIN AND YANG AND THE HEXAGRAMS

The hexagrams come from a total of 64 six-lined symbols that make up the *I Ching – the Book of Changes*. The *I Ching*, China's most important book, goes back to mythical antiquity. Nearly all that is great and significant in the cultural history of China can be traced to it, and it is also a book of divination. The three hexagrams highlighted in this chapter – chien, kun, and sheng – are the three luckiest hexagrams of the *I Ching*. In themselves they are good fortune symbols that bring auspicious luck to households.

TO ATTRACT PLENTY OF YANG ENERGY, OPEN ALL THE DRAPES SO THAT THE SUN CAN FLOOD INTO YOUR HOME.

CHIEN – THE CREATIVE

Chien is the first of the 64 hexagrams of the *I Ching*. It is the ultimate symbol of Yang energy. This hexagram comprises six unbroken lines as shown on the right.

Chien creates light, giving active and spirited Chi, which attracts great good fortune. Chien is also said to bring luck from heaven, whose essence is power.

Chien benefits the patriarch of the family, the natural leader or breadwinner. It is best placed in the northwest of the house or living room. This is indicated by the Later Heaven Arrangement of the trigrams around the Pa Kua symbol (*see* the illustration on page 24). By placing images of the chien hexagram in the northwest,

the luck of sublime success is created. This will be fueled by the full power of heaven, therefore implying great strength. The capacity represented by the hexagram chien is creative, and it is at its zenith during the summer months when the full benefits will be felt.

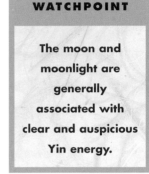

The best way to simulate this hexagram is to incorporate it into the design of lines on ceilings, walls, and furniture. If you find it difficult to incorporate six lines you can also try using three lines because this is often sufficient for activating the chien symbol.

If your main door is located in the northwest sector of your home, or it is directly facing the northwest direction, it is a very good idea to "carve" or emboss the image of chien onto your main door.

This benefits the Feng Shui of the whole household, but in particular it benefits the Feng Shui of the breadwinner of the family. Meanwhile, if the main bedroom is located in the northwest sector of the house, incorporating solid lines onto ceiling and wall cornices activates the chien energy.

THE CHIEN HEXAGRAM IS THE FIRST OF THE 64 HEXAGRAMS OF THE "I CHING". IT IS THE ULTIMATE SYMBOL OF YANG ENERGY.

ACTIVATING THE KUN HEXAGRAM WILL
BENEFIT THE MATRIARCH OF THE HOUSEHOLD.

KUN – THE RECEPTIVE

Kun encapsulates all the earth energy. Thus where chien is heaven, kun signifies the earth; and where chien is the patriarch, kun manifests the essence of the matriarch. This hexagram stands for the ultimate Yin energy. It is female where chien is male; and it is made up of six broken lines (*see* right) where chien is made up of six unbroken lines.

The place of kun is the southwest, as indicated in the Yang Pa Kua arrangement of trigrams (*see* page 24). Its element is big earth. Thus kun benefits from powerful earth energy. Activating this hexagram will benefit the females of the family, and in particular the matriarch or dowager of the household. It is an especially excellent Feng Shui enhancer for widows who have to transform themselves into the family breadwinner.

Activate kun by incorporating the symbol of broken lines into furniture and wall designs in the sector of the southwest. When you complement this with other earth energizers in this sector the luck created is most auspicious. The hexagram brings sublime success, usually brought about through the perseverance of the mother. It ensures a smooth progress of all projects that benefit the family undertaken by the matriarch.

Energizing the kun hexagram is also extremely beneficial for relationship luck. Friends can be found from all the eight directions and especially from the four cardinal directions of the compass. These will be friends you can count on. Likewise, those people wishing for luck associated with matters of the heart can energize the southwest with images of the kun hexagram. Carve the symbol onto a table in the southwest, and then shine a bright light on it. Combining the fire element with that of kun creates a wonderful balance of Yin Yang and also enhances the earth element since fire produces earth.

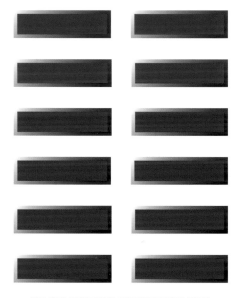

THE KUN HEXAGRAM: THE SIX BROKEN LINES
REPRESENT THE ULTIMATE IN YIN ENERGY.

SHENG – TO GROW UPWARD

The image opposite is hexagram number 46 – sheng, which is made up of the trigrams sun below and kun above. The image here is of wood inside the earth pushing upward, and the meaning is the attainment of a state of steady growth. It is a very auspicious hexagram because it implies inevitable and supreme success.

It also implies that your career path, as well as your path though life, will be relatively free of obstacles. There are few hindrances to achieving your aspirations.

Sheng implies that in the early stages of growth, initial impetus comes from your own confidence. Yet because it is early days, the hexagram also advises humility. Then help will come from all quarters. Sheng also implies obtaining the help and support of powerful patrons who notice your perseverance and hard work. In other words, you will also enjoy the luck of being recognized for your hard work by someone who can help you. This mentor luck continues as long as one is steady and continues to persevere. Because of the various layers of luck offered by the meaning of sheng, practitioners of the *I Ching* school of Feng Shui recommend placing this hexagram as a good luck symbol.

The hexagram combines two trigrams. The trigram sun is the wood below the ground. It pushes upward and grows into a large tree. The metaphor brings good fortune, and is expressed in the *I Ching* in this way:

"*Within the earth, wood grows*
The image of pushing upward
Thus the superior man of good character
Heaps up small things
To achieve something high and great."

Copy this hexagram and place it in the east or southeast – the sectors of the wood element – to harness its luck. If your main entrance door is located in either of these wood sectors it will be most beneficial to incorporate the hexagram into a door design. To attract auspicious energy, you can also draw the hexagram and place it above the doorway just inside the house.

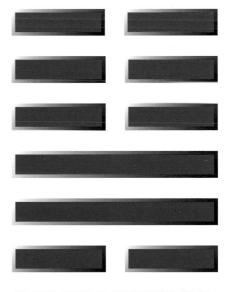

THE SHENG HEXAGRAM: THE TRIGRAM "SUN" SITS
BELOW THE TRIGRAM "KUN."

The Symbols of the *Wu Xing*

Categorized under the five elements – fire, wood, water, earth, and metal – are symbols that energize, strengthen, and magnify the direction or corner that corresponds to the element. Each sector is also identified with a different kind of luck. This is one of the simplest ways of strengthening the elements of corners with good fortune symbols.

There are groupings of symbols that are associated with each of the five elements. This association is based on the theory of *wu xing* or five elements, which is the most significant dimension to the understanding and interpretation of Feng Shui symbolism. *Wu xing* is the major principle on which both corrective and activating Feng Shui is based, and many symbols can be used either for correcting bad Feng Shui features or for activating good Feng Shui.

According to *wu xing*, everything in the universe – including the eight primary and secondary directions of the compass – can be categorized as belonging to one of the five elements – wood, fire, water, metal, and earth. Based on the laws of Feng Shui, these five elements have both a producing and a destroying cycle. When you apply these two dimensions of *wu xing* Feng Shui to your living or work space, you will realize two things:

1 There are a great number of creative and personalized methods that you can apply for creating good Feng Shui.

2 Why I keep saying Feng Shui can be as easy or as difficult as you want it to be.

Feng Shui does not have to be difficult to work but it must be based on sound fundamental principles. *Wu xing* is one of these basic fundamentals, and to use the theory in the practice of symbolic Feng Shui it is necessary to understand a few basic principles:

EACH ELEMENT IS ASSOCIATED WITH A PARTICULAR SECTOR OF THE HOME.

- First learn to identify good fortune objects.
- Next, practice categorizing these objects according to the five elements.
- Third, try to understand the nature and dimensions of the productive and destructive cycles of the five elements.

THE FIVE ELEMENTS AND THE PA KUA

The Pa Kua is the eight-sided octagonal symbol of Feng Shui analysis. Look at the Pa Kua shown on page 24 and note the trigrams. Since trigrams represent the root symbols of the *I Ching*, they are also considered the base symbols of Feng Shui. Each side or sector of the Pa Kua takes its Feng Shui meanings from the trigram that is placed there.

There are two special arrangements of the eight trigrams around the Pa Kua, the Early Heaven arrangement and the Later Heaven arrangement. While it is not necessary to enter into an academic treatise on why there are two different trigram arrangements, it is necessary to understand the nature of these differences, and to know which Pa Kua to use for what purpose.

The Yin Pa Kua (Early Heaven arrangement) is used mainly to undertake Feng Shui analysis of Yin dwellings for gravesite Feng Shui and in the application of some of the formulas of Flying Star time dimension Feng Shui. It is also used as a defensive tool against poison arrows. In this arrangement south is the place of ultimate Yang or heaven, while north is the place of ultimate Yin or earth.

The Yang Pa Kua (Later Heaven arrangement) is the one used exclusively for undertaking Feng Shui analysis of Yang dwellings – the houses of the living. Note the placement of each trigram. The three solid lines of the trigram chien, which represents the ultimate Yang energy, is in the northwest, while kun (the three broken lines and the trigram of ultimate Yin, matriarchal energy) is in the southwest. Carefully study the other trigrams and their respective placements. Note also the element attributes of each compass direction. Many recommendations are based on the element associations of the directions.

EVERYTHING IN THE UNIVERSE BELONGS
TO ONE OF THE FIVE ELEMENTS –
WATER, WOOD, EARTH, METAL, OR FIRE.

ELEMENTS AND COMPASS DIRECTIONS

Matching the elements and attributes to each of the compass directions creates the basis for symbolic Feng Shui. All symbols have Chi energies that derive from what they are made of and where they are placed. Understanding this can help create maximum benefits out of their display and usage.

The Yang Pa Kua symbol illustrated here reveals the rings of symbolic meanings applicable in each of the eight sectors. These offer clues on how to use the traditional symbols of good fortune to enhance home decor. For instance, if you wish to energize the east sector of your home, note this is the place of the trigram chen, which represents the eldest son, big wood, Yang energy, thunder, and all the feelings associated with arousing. Thus things made of wood are suitable. All colors associated with this element are also suitable, so greens and browns would enhance this part of the house. In addition, the shape associated with the wood element is rectangular, so this shape is good for this corner. In terms of celestial creatures, the east is the place of the dragon. Male and Yang energies in this corner are strong – if they are in excess, cool down excessive Yang with water, an element that is also in harmony with the wood element.

If the east corner is missing in your home or a room of your home, then all attributes associated with this location are deemed to be missing.

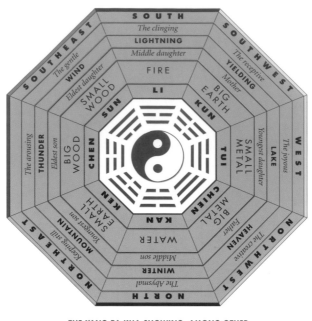

THE YANG PA KUA SHOWING, AMONG OTHER THINGS, THE TRIGRAMS AND ELEMENTS THAT CORRESPOND TO EACH DIRECTION.

When practicing symbolic Feng Shui, figure out the attributes of each sector direction, paying particular attention to the relevant element of each sector.

Just making sure that the relevant element is properly energized is already a significant part of Feng Shui. Thus, when you place an auspicious symbol in any corner, try to use an image that is in harmony with the element of the sector. This requires knowledge of the destructive and productive cycles of the elements. This is a whole subject in its own right (*see* the books described on page 42), but here is an example to show what can be achieved.

The example illustrated here is wood producing fire. An image like this would enhance the fire element of the south corner, if that is what you wish to do.

On the other hand, this symbol can also exhaust the wood corners of east and southeast if these corners were for some reason afflicted, and you needed to change this.

WOOD COMBINED WITH FIRE ENHANCES THE SOUTH CORNER, WHOSE ASSOCIATE ELEMENT IS FIRE.

DESIGN MOTIFS AND PATTERNS

These can vary according to shapes relating to the five elements. When used correctly, patterns and motifs that reflect the five elements can strengthen the energy of these elements. The matching of element with pattern or design is one of the easiest and most effective ways of

MOUNTAINS OR HILLS OFFER SUPPORT TO A HOME IF THEY ARE BEHIND IT.

magnifying the positive energies of the sectors of your living and work spaces. The sectors are identified according to the elements.

Shown on this page are four patterns that appear in wallpaper prints, on drapes, and as tile designs. By understanding the element association of design motifs, it is possible to work them into interior decoration ideas. The water motif below looks like an ocean wave and the bubbles indicate Yang water: water that has life. This design would be excellent for any corner that benefits from water (north, southeast, and east). This motif is great in black and blue and is ideal for restaurants, wine bars, and pubs.

The square maze design suggests the element of earth since the square symbol stands for earth. Ideally,

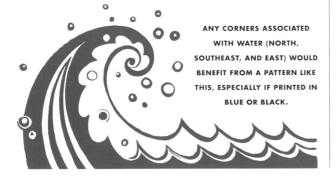

ANY CORNERS ASSOCIATED WITH WATER (NORTH, SOUTHEAST, AND EAST) WOULD BENEFIT FROM A PATTERN LIKE THIS, ESPECIALLY IF PRINTED IN BLUE OR BLACK.

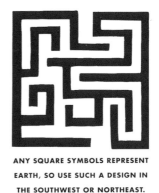

ANY SQUARE SYMBOLS REPRESENT EARTH, SO USE SUCH A DESIGN IN THE SOUTHWEST OR NORTHEAST.

it is suitable for the earth corners of the home, which are the southwest and the northeast. It is also excellent for rooms located at the heart of the home. A square motif is suited for industries and business engaged in property and real estate.

ROUND MOTIFS REPRESENT METAL, SO USE A PATTERN LIKE THIS IN THE WEST OR NORTHWEST.

The round motif is suitable for the metallic corners of the home: the west or northwest. The pattern also denotes a precious stone, which has an auspicious meaning since precious stones are akin to metal – being mined from mother earth. This symbol is thus considered auspicious in metal corners.

The mountain range is suggestive of support for the house. Placed in the back half of the home, it creates protective Chi. But it also suggests big earth, so something like this when placed in the southwest corner of the home would create Chi that is beneficial to the mother, as well as enhance and smooth all family and sibling relationships.

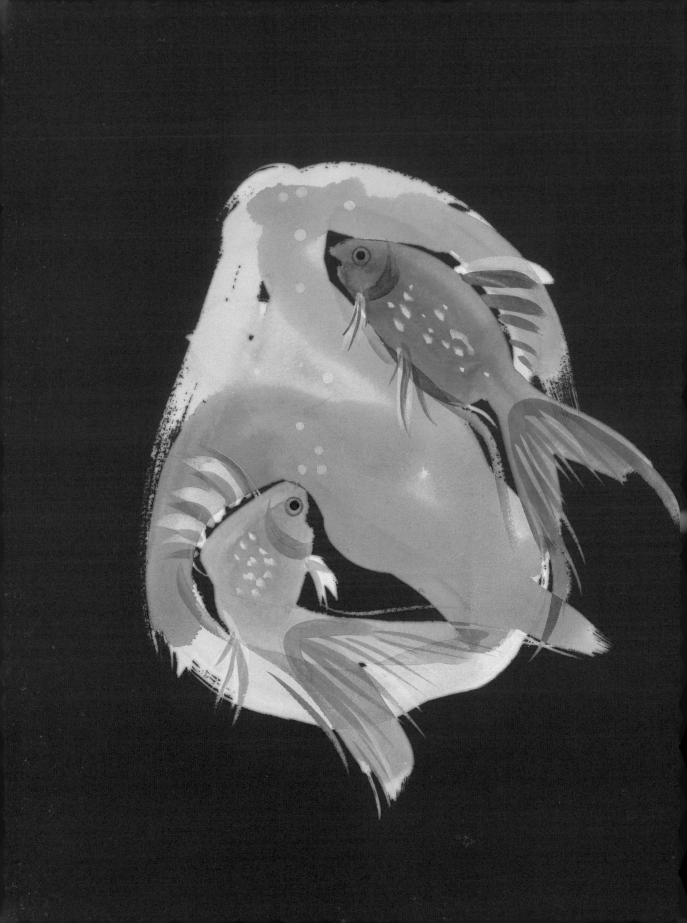

1

SYMBOLS OF WEALTH AND SUCCESS

Make liberal use of good fortune coins to enhance and attract the Chi of wealth to your business ventures. Simulate the merchant ship laden with cargo, bringing wealth into your home; learn to create wealth vases and bowls. Keep three-legged toads, bats, and arrowanas to activate the Yang of prosperity. Create a goldfish paradise, and use the most magnificent symbol of all – the mighty and celestial dragon – its alter ego the phoenix, and all the other creatures of good fortune – the chi lin, the dragon horse, the dragon tortoise. Place these and other symbols of prosperity in a Feng Shui orientation and bring wealth energy into your home.

Authentic Good Fortune Coins

Chinese coins represent the powerful union of heaven and earth. Described as being "square within and round without," these round coins, usually made of copper, have been used as metal currency from the T'ai Kung in the eleventh century B.C.E. The square shape in the center is the energy of the earth, while the circle represents the Chi of heaven. Combined, they drive the power of wealth luck, and when energized with a red string, Yang energy breathes precious life into them, transforming them into powerful emblems of wealth and prosperity. Coins taken from a rich person's home possess an abundance of wealth energy, and the nine emperor coins that represent the reign of nine emperors of a single dynasty denote continued wealth for nine generations.

Those eager to do so may spend some time "treasure hunting" for authentic antique coins from the various Chinese dynasties. The Chinese characters on the coins usually bear the name of the reign. When you have collected coins from nine emperors' reigns, tie them together with a red thread and hang them on the wall behind you at work. This means you have the financial support of nine emperors and is believed to be most auspicious. I believe that these coins should ideally be chosen from the reign periods that represent periods of prosperity. Thus coins from the Emperor Chien Lung's period or from the Kang Hsi period will be better than from the closing days of the Ching Dynasty. The wu chu or tael coin of the Han Dynasty (206 B.C.E. to 25 C.E.) is considered to be one of the luckiest and most decorative objects of prosperity. The wu chu coin has been reproduced in gold, silver, bronze, and jade to be worn around the neck on a chain or cord for a long time, but the genuine wu chu coin is very rare.

According to Chinese scholars some of the old antique coins were believed to be so powerful in attracting wealth luck that families would let their sons wear these coins around their necks as good luck amulets. The provincial coins of the Kang Hsi period, for example, bearing characters on Yang and Yin sides, are believed to have talismanic powers when strung together with red thread or hung around the neck on a gold chain. Coins of the Chien Lung period are also held in high esteem.

For Feng Shui purposes, some of the provincial cities of China were said to have deities of wealth at the city gates, and nine coins strung together with red thread would be hung around the neck of these deities of wealth to attract good fortune.

For modern-day usage, the gold and diamond equivalent of the coins are a suitable substitute. The use

> **WATCHPOINT**
>
> **Tie coins from nine emperors' reigns together with red thread and hang them on the wall behind you at work for strong financial luck and support.**

of genuine precious materials such as gold and diamonds bring the ultimate Chi energy to the coins. In addition, it is also possible to wear rings and earrings, cufflinks and tie pins, all fashioned with these diamond and gold copies of this old symbol. The ideal number of coins to wear on the body is nine coins, thus a ring with a pair of earrings, each with three coins, or a necklace with a pair of earrings would be ideal.

COINS WORN AS PROTECTIVE AMULETS

As well as bringing prosperity, these good fortune coins are also used as protective amulets. For example, take nine coins from the Chien Lung period (either the genuine old coins or gold/jade imitations are acceptable) and tie them with red string to hang around the neck of a deity of wealth for 7, 14, or 21 days. This symbolically empowers the coins with auspicious Chi and thus they acquire potency. The coins can then be worn around the neck of a child to overcome the 30 dangerous barriers of a person's life. The number of coins hung around the neck must equal the age of the child (in the Chinese statement of age please add one year); and each year a fresh coin is added during the first day of the lunar New Year until the child attains the age of 15 years. By that time the child is believed to have symbolically and successfully crossed all the barriers along the path of life.

These barriers are those of the four seasons, the four pillars, the demon cow king, the devil's gate demon, the insurmountable difficulties, the golden hen falling into a well, and the barrier of the private parts. Then there

> **WATCHPOINT**
>
> Place "knife" coins in afflicted corners that threaten the loss of wealth of the family.

are the barriers of the hundred days: the broken bridge, the nimble foot, the five genii, the golden padlock, the iron snake, the bathing tub, the white tiger, and the Buddhist monks.

Finally, there are the barriers posed by the heavenly dog, that of invoking heaven's pity and those associated with the lock and key, where the bowels are sundered and where the head is broken. These create the barriers of the thousand days: of the nocturnal weeping, of the burning broth, of the time when children are buried, where life is shortened, caused by the general's dagger, deep running water, or fire and water.

Over time, the use of these coin amulets became superstitious, and the coins worn around the neck evolved into clusters of coins tied to resemble swords, decorated with knots and tassels. Coins used for warding off Shar Chi, or killing breath, are known as *pi hsieh chien*. These knife coins (whose origin goes back to the first century) are believed to make excellent antidotes for Feng Shui afflicted corners that threaten the loss of wealth of the family. Place them in the corners of your home that give you problems.

COINS FOR SHOP DOORS

Hang two coins tied with red thread over shop doors. They will attract wealth to the establishment. The potency of this symbol is said to equal that of the God of Riches. Place the coins directly above the main entrance door and refresh them each year on the first day of the lunar New Year. It is believed that for this purpose the genuine Chien Lung or Ching Dynasty coins are extraordinarily potent.

COINS TO INCREASE
YOUR BUSINESS

Stick three coins tied with red thread onto your important files and invoice books to increase your business. Since it can be difficult to find genuine antique Chinese coins, the cottage entrepreneurs of China and Taiwan have now come out with really good copies of Ching Dynasty coins, some of which even look like real gold! If you find an inexpensive source, do as I do and buy a couple of hundred. Usually they cost about a dollar for three. It is not necessary for the coins to be genuinely old. The power of the coins comes from their shape and meaning, not from their age. Stick the coins onto all your important files, order books, and cash boxes, in your safe and inside your pocketbook or wallet. The physical presence of three coins made energetic with the addition of red thread is said to attract wealth luck wherever they are placed. I have them on my doorknobs and stuck to my fax machine and computer. This brings loads of wonderful opportunities communicated to me by fax and e-mail.

WEAR A JADE PIECE ON A RED THREAD TO IMPROVE YOUR GOOD FORTUNE.

Note that when you stick coins on your files and fax machines and so forth, the Yang side must be uppermost. This is the side with the four Chinese words; the side with the two characters is the Yin side. I keep lots of coins in my home, all tied with red thread so I always have stock to give to someone who needs them. This is one of the simplest and most effective of Feng Shui tips and has benefited many people.

COINS TO ENHANCE
THE WEALTH OF A MARRIAGE

In the *Imperial Record of Chinese Coins* it was recorded that there is a certain form of coin-shaped talisman known as "coins for throwing into the bed chamber," which are believed to bring great wealth to the couple and also many successful children. The story here is that one of the emperors of the Tang Dynasty was advised by his Feng Shui master to have coins fashioned of gold and silver thrown onto the marriage bed of his favorite daughter. These gold coins were engraved with various auspicious phrases. It is also reported that the Emperor Wu of the Han Dynasty and his consort were very superstitious so they arranged to be showered with gold and silver coins each time they rested on the royal couch. This was based on the belief that the coins would bring lots of descendants' luck to the dynasty and bless them with many sons.

To strengthen the luck of young married couples, therefore, take a leaf out of these Imperial records. In the old days, emperors had access to the best Feng Shui brains of the country.

A very popular good fortune symbol favored by Chinese mothers is a round disklike jade pendant with a hole in the center. This is worn around the neck for good luck and protection. It is believed that the soft smoothness of jade combined with the coin shape are extremely auspicious. A variation of this is the ten jade pieces tied together with red thread. This is similar in effect to the ten emperor coins.

COMBINING COINS WITH OTHER
SYMBOLS OF GOOD FORTUNE

Good fortune coins can be combined with almost all the animal symbols of good fortune. Combined with the bat, the meaning is "good fortune now." Combined with two magpies, the meaning is "may one see good fortune before one's eyes;" and combined with the cow, *chi lin*, sheep, mongoose, tortoise, or dragon, the connotations of wealth and success are multiplied a thousand times over. An animal sitting or standing on a bed of coins represents abundance and plenty.

GOLD INGOTS ON A MERCHANT SHIP

One of the most popular symbols of business success leading to the accumulation of wealth that was favored by the Chinese merchant traders in Southeast Asia during the turn of the century was the merchant ship. Many used the junk or the sailing ship laden with cargo as their business logo with great success.

- You can create a symbolic wealth ship piled high with gold ingots to attract higher income and success to your business.
- These gold ingots need not be real.
- Get a dozen imitation gold ingots from Chinatown and go searching for a wooden sailing ship or trader's junk about 12in (30cm) long.
- Fill the model ship's hold with the ingots. Let it overflow onto the deck. For it to have really good meaning, the ship must be laden with gold.
- Next place the model ship inside your office, preferably in the foyer area. Position the ship so it looks like it is sailing around inside and not about to sail out through the door.
- If the ship is sailing outward you will lose money. Let it seem as if the wind is strongly blowing the ship into harbor. Wherever the ship is placed, there will be the harbor. Let your office be the harbor. Or you can also place a ship in your house, preferably on a low table.

USE MORE THAN ONE GOLD-LADEN MERCHANT SHIP TO REPRESENT DIFFERENT SOURCES OF INCOME.

CREATING A WEALTH VASE

Vases are exceptionally auspicious symbols to have at home since they signify "perpetual peace and harmony in the home." This is because the phonetic sound of the vase is "ping," which also means peace. The vase is also one of the eight auspicious signs of Buddhism, being one of the objects found on the footprints of Buddha.

To create a wealth vase, choose a vase made of porcelain, crystal, earthenware, or metal (bronze, silver, or even gold). It should have a fairly wide mouth, a slender neck, and a wide bottom. This symbolizes plenty of wealth flowing in, and once it flows down the narrow neck, it stays inside the large base of the vase signifying that wealth will stay in the family for a long long time.

If the vase is decorated with auspicious wealth symbols such as the dragon or the red bat, it is even better. A vase that has the four season flowers (see page 84) will signify that your family will have wealth and harmony through the year. A vase decorated with dragons and phoenixes benefits the whole family.

To create a treasure vase (referred to as the *pao ping* or rare vase), fill the vase to its brim with the following objects and keep it hidden from view:

- Seven types of semiprecious stones. Choose from crystal, coral, lapis, pearl, jasper, cornelian, quartz, tiger eye, aquamarine, topaz, amethyst, citrine, and malachite.
- A bit of soil from a rich person's house. You will have to be ingenious about this. Don't steal. Ask for it. Soil that is given to you is very lucky.
- A red package filled with real money.
- Three, six, or nine Chinese coins that have each been tied with red thread (optional).
- Five types of "nourishing fruits" (seeds or grain) to signify plenty to eat at all times. Some say this also guarantees good descendants' luck. This can be millet, dates, wheat, barley, sorghum, red beans, green beans, or soybeans. Place in a small plastic bag (optional).

The Three-Legged Toad

The three-legged toad is probably the most auspicious symbol for enhancing prosperity. There are several myths associated with the origins of this belief. In fact, according to Chinese mythology, the three-legged toad is said to live on the moon, which it succeeds in swallowing during an eclipse. As a result, it is sometimes said to signify the unattainable.

An extension of the myth outlined above is that the wife of one of the Eight Immortals stole the elixir of immortality from the Queen of the West, Hsi Wang Mu. She fled to the moon where she was turned into a toad. But having tasted the elixir she had attained immortality and in the midst of being changed into a toad she had begged for mercy. The gods, ever compassionate, softened, so only the upper half of the body took the form of the ugly creature. Instead of the hindquarters, the gods allowed the retention of the tail of the tadpole.

In a related legend, the mythical three-legged toad is being baited with gold coins by Lui Hai, one of the Eight Immortals, a Minister of State who lived during the tenth century C.E. Lui Hai was believed to be proficient in Taoist magic and had knowledge of the toad's powers for attracting wealth and prosperity.

After much searching for this mythical creature, Lui Hai found it hiding deep inside a well. Aware of the toad's fondness for money, he is said to have baited the creature to come up from the well. As bait he used a

A TYPICAL THREE-LEGGED TOAD. PLACE IT INSIDE YOUR HOME ON A LOW TABLE.

red line tied with gold coins. This has resulted in the painting of a child baiting the three-legged toad with coins tied on a long red string to become an emblem meaning that wealth is about to come to the lucky individual.

The legend of the three-legged toad as an auspicious symbol of wealth thus originated from the popular representation of Lui Hai, who stood one foot resting on the toad and held in his hand a red string on which five gold coins were strung. This image was said to be most auspicious and conducive to attracting great good fortune. Since then, the three-legged toad with a coin in its mouth has become the symbol for attracting wealth and prosperity.

Over time the legend grew, and today decorative representations of the three-legged toad show it sitting on a bed of coins and ingots and always with a coin in its mouth. However, Lui Hai the Immortal has mysteriously vanished from the image. Fake toads are best when made of any one of the semiprecious stones such as aventurine or jasper.

FROGS AND TOADS

The Chinese do not distinguish very clearly between the frog and the toad. But they do believe that the spawn of the frog falls from heaven, like dew, and that the spittle resembling white juice from the toad can be used very effectively as medicine for all kinds of forehead, throat, and heart ailments. Infirmities associated with these three upper chakra centers of the body are believed to be hard to cure, and a dried version of the toad's spittle is said to be a good cure for such ailments. This can be bought from Chinese medicine shops. It is also very good medicine for those who smoke.

THE CHINESE BELIEVE THAT FROG SPAWN IS A GIFT FROM HEAVEN.

WHERE TO PLACE THE THREE-LEGGED TOAD

There seems to be some confusion on the best position, location, and orientation of the toad for it to be most beneficial. I place the three-legged toad near my main front door so that it is positioned fairly low but not on the ground. Coffee table level is about right.

I do not recommend placing the toad directly in front of the door. The best place is in one of the corners, diagonally opposite; the toad should be looking at the door as though expecting to greet the wealth Chi. There are those who say that the toad should face the door during daylight and be turned to face inward during nighttime. I believe this is because occasionally it is good for the toad to look into the home.

You can place as many three-legged toads in your home or office as you wish. I have them all over my living room, dining room, and also in my garden, hidden between rocks near my small fish ponds and waterfall garden. But the total number of toads in my house never exceeds nine. If you are like me and wish to have these toads all around your house, do be discreet in your display of them and only keep them in the public areas of your home. In other words, I recommend that you should not keep them in bedrooms and kitchens. Energizing for wealth in the bedroom disturbs your sleep, and in the kitchen it has the opposite effect.

TRADITIONAL CHINESE MEDICINE CURES INCLUDE A DRIED VERSION OF TOAD'S SPITTLE.

Fish in Water

The fish is a popular emblem of wealth because the Chinese character for fish, *yu*, also means abundance. During the lunar New Year, the word *sarng* is added to it to imply growth in abundance. The exchange of gifts of live fish indicates the significant goodwill of friends and relatives.

If you wish to activate the good fortune symbolism of fish in water, it is best to consider keeping some of the more popular of the good fortune fish. These are carp, goldfish, and arrowana, but essentially any brightly colored or red fish are believed to signify good fortune. If you are thinking of keeping an aquarium of arrowanas, a pond of carp, or a bowl of goldfish, here are some useful tips to help you make the best of your water feature:

- Always place your water feature in the south-east, east, or north of your home, apartment, or garden. Do not do so if these sectors happen to fall into one of your bedrooms since water in the bedroom causes loss and is not recommended.
- Always keep the water well oxygenated and clean since this generates the precious and wealth-bringing Yang energy that you want. It also ensures your fish remain healthy.
- If any of your fish die for no apparent reason, give all the remaining fish a bath of appropriate medicine and replace the dead fish with new ones. Do not worry about a fish dying but say a silent prayer for its departed soul, for it, too, was once a living being. Fish that die are believed to have helped you avoid some specific misfortune.

- Make sure your water feature is neither too large nor too small. Balance is vital. If it is too small it might not be as effective and if it is too large, the excess of water could cause problems. Too much water is harmful.
- In terms of the number of fish to keep, multiples of nine are a good guide. But if you are keeping arrowanas, a single arrowana in the north sector is the most potent. If you want to keep more, five is a good number. In addition to generating good wealth Feng Shui, the arrowana is also an auspicious symbol of protection.
- Make sure you do not mix your fish. The arrowana, for instance, will devour all other fish. The goldfish will have its beautiful tail fins destroyed by the carp, and the carp and the arrowana simply cannot coexist side by side.

THE ARROWANA OR DRAGON FISH

In recent years, the tropical arrowana or dragon fish has become increasingly popular as a powerful Feng Shui energizer of wealth luck. This exceptionally beautiful fish comes in many different varieties. The shape and color of arrowanas vary according to where they originate, and it is only those varieties that show a tinge of pink, gold, or silver that are the prized specimens with good Feng Shui connotations. If the fish does not show scales that have a silvery sheen, they are regarded as poor relations of the real thing. Thus those people who wish to keep the arrowana should be careful. The fish are also expensive, both to buy and to maintain, since they generally feed on live fish, shrimp, or worms.

I kept five arrowanas in the late 1980s to capture much needed prosperity luck for myself, and after the fish had brought me the fortune I needed to retire from corporate life I released them into the Stanley reservoir of Hong Kong. But I have since felt great regret at having fed them a diet of live goldfish. If I were to keep them again I would train them to eat special fish pellets. This is not easy to do since arrowanas are very fussy in their diet. But I do urge you to try, since feeding them live bait is not good for one's karma. I have now changed to keeping goldfish instead.

A SINGLE ARROWANA KEPT IN THE NORTH SECTOR OF YOUR HOME ATTRACTS GOOD WEALTH CHI.

THE GOLDFISH

The goldfish is the all-time favorite symbol for excellent wealth Feng Shui. The two words that mean goldfish are also the two words that phonetically mean gold and abundance. The word *kum* is gold and the word *yu* means fish and it also means abundance. Thus, *kum yu* means gold in abundance. For this reason the Chinese have always been very fond of keeping goldfish in their homes.

To use the goldfish to enhance your wealth Feng Shui, it is a good idea to go for varieties that look fat and prosperous and are red or gold in color. Thus the specially developed Japanese ryukins, which are a bright red, are an excellent choice. The lion-headed Chinese varieties that have white silver scales and a bright red head are also excellent. Keep eight of these Yang colored fish together with a single one of the black variety. Choose a black goldfish that swims vigorously and is completely black with no other markings.

This combination of eight Yang-colored fish with one Yin-colored fish will ensure not just prosperity but also protection against loss and being cheated. The total number of nine represents the fullness of heaven and earth. If you wish to keep more than nine goldfish, ensure that you only keep them in multiples of nine.

Keep your goldfish in an aquarium, or better yet in a goldfish bowl so that you look down onto the fish from the top. If you place oxygenators into the water, the bubbles in the water keep it energized with Yang energy. It is also a good idea to have a filter to ensure the water stays clean.

Place this auspicious water feature in the north part of your home or garden for maximum good luck. Or place it in the east or southeast. Do not place live goldfish in water in the south part of your home. In the south, goldfish do more harm than good.

COLORED FISH

The fish has always been an emblem of wealth and abundance, not just because of the phonetics of the word *yu*, but also because fish is always in such plentiful supply. Due to its awesome reproductive powers, it is also a symbol of fertility, and because it swims happily in its own environment, it has become an emblem of connubial bliss and harmony.

In the old days, a fish was almost always included as one of the items in the betrothal gifts given to the parents of the bride. This was due to its auspicious significance. In addition, a pair of fish was also noted for being emblematic of

the joys of union, particularly of a sexual nature. The fish emblem was also believed to be an effective charm against bad luck since it is included among the auspicious signs on the footprints of the Buddha.

The double fish symbol is regarded as one of the Buddhist auspicious objects (*see* pages 112–115) and is usually embroidered onto door curtains and pillowcases for good luck. The double fish symbol is an amulet said to possess strong protective energies as well as an enhancer of the good Sheng Chi, worn to attract good luck. In Thailand, children are often given the double fish symbol to wear around their necks. These are usually made of gold, and sometimes set with precious stones such as rubies, sapphires, and emeralds.

PLENTY OF AIR BUBBLES IN THE WATER INTRODUCE STRONG YANG ENERGY TO THE HOME.

Modern-day jewelry designs of the double fish symbol set with diamonds and gold are also worn by superstitious rich ladies who believe that the double fish symbol protects them from being cast aside by their husbands for younger women.

The carp is also a good fortune symbol, suggestive of martial attributes. The carp is known for its legendary valor in swimming against the current to reach the Dragon Gate (also known as the *lung men*) and thus become a dragon. The legend of the dragon carp has it that the sturgeons of the Yellow River made the ascent of the stream during the third moon of each year in an attempt to pass above the rapids of the *lung men*. In this way, they were transformed into dragons. It has made the carp a symbol of perseverance and literary and educational success.

If you wish your sons or daughters to excel in their examinations and become "straight A" students, keep lots of carp in a pond inside the house. The carp seldom fails to deliver.

HERE IS A PICTURE OF THE CARP POND IN MY HOME. IT IS LOCATED ON THE LEFT-HAND SIDE OF MY FRONT DOOR. I HAVE HAD THIS POND FOR OVER 20 YEARS.

The Dragon and the Phoenix

These celestial creatures are symbols of success and prosperity. They are the ultimate Yang and Yin symbols of Chinese cosmology and mythology. The dragon is the symbol of male vigor and fertility; and the phoenix symbolizes Yin splendor and female beauty when placed with the dragon. Alone, however, the phoenix takes on Yang characteristics and male essence, thereby symbolizing other attributes. Together the dragon and phoenix also symbolize the emperor and empress, and the happiness of marital union.

The presence of the dragon and phoenix together in any home always symbolizes a fruitful marriage that is blessed with success and prosperity as well as many male offspring. This is the principal reason behind the dragon and the phoenix being such a popular symbol for marriage celebrations and especially during the tea drinking ceremony.

The union of these two symbolic creatures at wedding festivities suggests a match that is blessed with plentiful money and descendants' luck. It denotes the beginning of the dynastic family with the dragon signifying the patriarch and the phoenix signifying the matriarch. Hung as a painting on the northwest wall it favors the patriarch's luck. Hung on the southwest wall it favors the matriarch's luck. Hung on the east wall it benefits the health of the family. Hung on the south wall it brings plenty of opportunities and recognition for the family.

USING THE DRAGON TO ACCUMULATE COSMIC CHI

The dragon is said to be the most powerfully potent symbol of good fortune in the Chinese pantheon of symbols. As one of the four creatures of the world's directions and as the principal symbol of Feng Shui, the dragon stands for new beginnings. It is the standard bearer of the east, the place where the sun rises and where the spring rains originate.

The dragon is the powerful emblem of rain, which brings water to the land. Thus it signifies the good water, which in turn is symbolic of wealth. It is also an expression of continuing success, great attainments, and prosperity. Because of this, there are no other symbols that can surpass it in popularity. Chinese businesses often incorporate the dragon into their company logo with long-lasting and great success.

Many businesses use the dragon symbol to create the precious cosmic Chi. It is this same Chi that brings good fortune to homes that enjoy good Feng Shui. Simulating the dragon inside the home energizes the luck of the dragon.

Place the dragon image in the living room of the home. Get ceramic, porcelain, or crystal dragons for the southwest and northeast corners of the room, and have wooden carved dragons for the east and southeast. In Feng Shui, the dragon will be beneficial wherever it is displayed. But to ensure it blends in well with the elements, especially note these locations. Also make certain it is not too large as to overwhelm the energies of the home: usually it is better to err on the side of its being too small. The best dragon replicas are those painted green or made from a green semiprecious stone.

Examples of good mediums are aventurine and jade, but since these are expensive, carved wooden dragons are also effective in simulating its presence. Place it at eye level: it should never be positioned too high since this means it will get out of control. Remember that you are in charge, not the dragon!

INVOKE THE POWER OF THE NINE DRAGONS

The mainland overlooking Hong Kong is called Kowloon, which means Nine Dragons, and Feng Shui masters are always quick to point to the prosperity of this abode of the nine mighty dragons. The potency of the Nine Dragons is given prominence and manifested by the presence of an exceptionally grand Nine Dragon ceramic wall placed in the Forbidden City in Beijing. This screen is brick, faced with a marvelous design of glazed colored tiles set in the form of nine coiling, writhing dragons. They are exceptionally beautiful and look very alive, seemingly ready to fend off all attacks by killing spirits and negative killing breath. This screen symbolizes all the dragons in existence (*see* the box to the right describing the power of each dragon) and is thus a protective screen.

Later, an exact replica was built and placed in Heibei Park in the city. Then in the mid-1980s, when Hong Kong was going through the throes of nervousness arising from the impending handover to China, a third Nine Dragon screen was erected on Hong Kong island facing the harbor and Kowloon. These colorful ceramic screens were all placed to tap into the tremendous good fortune and protection associated with the Nine Dragons, each of whom have particular protective attributes.

THE NINE DRAGONS

1	**P'u-lao**	alerts and protects when there is danger. He is the dragon carved on bells, gongs, and singing bowls.
2	**Ch'iu-niu**	creates Yang energy with music.
3	**Pi-his**	brings the luck of knowledge and education.
4	**Pa-hsia**	brings support and strength.
5	**Chao-feng**	guards temples and other holy places.
6	**Chih wen**	symbolizes the power of water over fire.
7	**Suan-ni**	protects from loss and betrayals.
8	**Yai-tzu**	protects from physical harm.
9	**Pi-kau**	protects against litigation.

If you can obtain a photograph or print of the Nine Dragon ceramic screen, hanging it near the vicinity of the front door invokes the good Chi of the Nine Dragons that benefit and protect all residents of the house. This is irrespective of the compass directions since the Nine Dragons represent the fullness of both heaven and earth, and by implication all the eight primary and secondary directions of the compass.

ENERGIZING WITH THE IMAGE OF THE DRAGON

The most powerful of all the dragons are the heaven dragons, which are said to bring powerful success luck for the family patriarch. These should be differentiated from the earth dragons associated with Feng Shui.

The image of the dragon brings auspicious luck into the home and office and its image can be placed in any one of the cardinal directions because although it is affiliated with the east, the dragon is also linked to each of the cardinal directions. Having said this, the dragon is especially powerful in the east so I strongly recommend you decorate the east wall of your living room with images of the dragon.

The lunar New Year is a particularly good time to energize dragon symbolism with auspicious dragon dances and loud Yang energy. To enhance the Yang energies of your home invest in ceramics and porcelain ware that carry the dragon image. Or display a dragon image made of semiprecious stone and carrying a pearl. Energize the corners of the living or dining room rather than the sleeping quarters.

OPPORTUNITY LUCK AND THE CELESTIAL PHOENIX

The phoenix is one of the four celestial creatures of Feng Shui and is the king of all the winged creatures. This magnificent and legendary bird is analogous with good fortune that is associated with opportunity luck. It symbolizes resilience – rising from the ashes of loss and destitution to soar to great heights of success and prosperity. At its best, the phoenix brings amazing turnaround luck. Just when you think that all is lost, it opens new channels and opportunities in your work and career. On its own, the phoenix is a soaring Yang symbol. It is associated with the fiery energies of the south and is also the God of the Four Winds. Its place in the practice of Feng Shui is especially potent for those wanting to magnify their chances of success in all fields of endeavor.

If you place the phoenix image in your home, look for a high place – a shelf or cupboard – where it can stand in splendor, its body evoking the five human qualities that attract the good cosmic Chi:

- Its head signifies virtue.
- Its wings signify a sense of duty and responsibility.
- Its back stands for correct behavior.
- Its breast spells humanity and compassion.
- Its stomach indicates reliability.

These five qualities are also reflected in the five colors to be found in its feathers.

Place the phoenix image along the south wall or corner of your home or living room. If you cannot find an image of the phoenix, you can use any of the other beautifully feathered birds as substitutes – the peacock or the rooster – but the phoenix will be the best. Energizing the phoenix can also be done with porcelain and paintings.

For the last 15 years, I have had a crystal phoenix with specks of gold in its body. This was a limited

THE PHOENIX ON ITS OWN IS A YANG SYMBOL; COMBINED WITH THE DRAGON IT BECOMES YIN.

associated with the sun, with the warmth of summer, and with the happiness that comes when a good harvest has been gathered in.

For wealth, it is recommended that a cinnabar-colored phoenix should be placed high along the south wall. Such a symbol of wealth should be specially commissioned so that it is shown in all its magnificence.

It is often drawn gazing into a ball of fire and so is strongly associated with the Yang energies of the living. But this is only when it is displayed on its own.

When the phoenix is shown with the dragon it takes on its Yin form, and the joint symbol signifies marital happiness. A picture with the phoenix on the right and the dragon on the left symbolizes husband and wife. Place such a picture in the southwest corner of your bedroom if you want to find a mate.

Two phoenixes together also signify connubial inter-course but the connotations of such a representation refer more to homosexuality, described in the old texts as false male and empty female phoenix.

Sometimes this symbolism is depicted showing children carrying a vase with flowers and sitting on the back of the phoenix.

edition piece I received as a gift and I placed it in the south corner of my office when I first received it. It brought me plenty of opportunities on an almost continuous basis. Today I have "retired" it since I cannot cope with too many opportunities. Instead, I have placed it in the southwest of the family room to stimulate good harmonious luck for the family.

THE PHOENIX AND PEACE

The phoenix presence is always associated with times of peace and prosperity, and having the spirit of the phoenix in the home encourages the in-flow of harmonious and prosperous Chi. This celestial creature presides over the southern quadrant of the heavens, and in accordance with the fire trigram of the south, is

WATCHPOINT

A phoenix drawn with a peony represents young lovers.

HANG AN IMAGE OF THE PHOENIX ON THE SOUTH WALL OF YOUR LIVING ROOM FOR PEACE AND PROSPERITY.

Other Symbolic Animals

Of the other creatures of good fortune, two are particularly potent in terms of their protective powers and meaning. The first is the dragon horse, which is excellent as a general protective symbol, and the second is the dragon tortoise, which also has the capability of overcoming bad Flying Stars.

THE CHINESE UNICORN

The mythical Chinese unicorn, known as *chi lin* in China, is sometimes referred to as the dragon horse. It is a fabulous creature of good omen, prosperity, success, longevity, illustrious offspring, and enchantment. The *chi lin* brings sons. Supposedly endowed with magical qualities, it is also associated with the Hou Tu square – an awesome symbol of numbers used in advanced Feng Shui analysis (*see* page 98). More, it is said to have emerged from the Yellow River bearing on its back the mystical map from which the legendary Fu Hsi (the founder of the *I Ching*) is said to have devised the written characters of the Chinese language. There are many legends and stories associated with the *chi lin* – almost all praising its many qualities, including its perfect goodwill, benevolence, and gentle nature.

The *chi lin*'s presence is said to attract the powerful cosmic breath of the dragon, thereby bringing good fortune luck to those residing in the abode. Since it is also regarded as a happy portent, the *chi lin* is believed to be an auspicious symbol to display at the work place. Place its image on your desk to stimulate the good attributes of this magnificent creature.

The *chi lin* is also believed to represent good fortune in promotions for those wanting advancement in their careers, and is especially lucky for those who work in the military. The *chi lin* is the symbol of the first rank military official, and its image can be found embroidered on court robes.

THE CHINESE UNICORN – OR *CHI LIN* – IS ALSO KNOWN AS THE DRAGON HORSE AND IS THE FOCUS OF MANY LEGENDS.

THE DRAGON TORTOISE

If you examine a live tortoise carefully, you will see that it has the head of a snake and a very long neck, which many people suggest resembles a dragon. Thus, embodied in this creature that still walks the face of the earth is the spirit of the dragon. Inside their homes, Feng Shui practitioners often display the dragon tortoise, frequently fashioned sitting on a bed of coins and gold ingots, as a symbol of great good fortune. In its mouth is a single coin of a prosperous reign period such as that of the Emperor Kangsu or the Emperor Chien Lung. Such a symbol embodies both the bravery of the dragon and the shielding qualities of the tortoise. Like the *chi lin*, this is a creature of the imagination and it demonstrates the way the Chinese use symbolism to enhance the physical space of their living environment.

There are multiple meanings to the image of the dragon tortoise, such as those given in the box below.

Such tortoises are easy to find in Chinese curio shops and supermarkets in Chinatown. They should not be expensive and are usually made of plaster painted with gold paint or they are made of brass and can be quite heavy. Displaying one is sufficient. There is no need to overdo the imagery by having too many of this creature.

You can use this symbol as a paperweight. Place it on your desk either in the north or east sector but not if this is directly in front of you. In Feng Shui, when you confront a powerful symbol you are asking for trouble. Instead, try to have it by the side of you. You can also place this symbol behind where you sit to signify that you have the support of both the dragon and the tortoise. Business people who place this image behind them at the office will find the business risks they take will be bolder, yet less risky. The bed of coins on which it rests indicates the successful accumulation of wealth and prosperity.

THE SYMBOLISM OF THE DRAGON TORTOISE

- The tortoise symbolizes longevity. Here is a creature that is reputed to be able to live to 3,000 years without food or air.
- The dragon symbolizes success, courage, and determination. That the tortoise has transformed into a dragon indicates impending good fortune in your career and business endeavors.
- The base of gold ingots upon which the creature sits signifies tremendous wealth and prosperity.
- The coin in its mouth signifies increased income.
- The baby tortoise on its back symbolizes wonderful descendants' luck, which usually means many sons.

THE TRIBUTE HORSE

The Chinese always associate the tribute horse with gifts given to emperors and other powerful court officials. From the times of the Sung emperors through to the Imperial rulers of the Qing Dynasty, the tribute horse has been associated with gifts brought by the vanquished to the victors. Thus the tribute horse symbolizes the spoils of battle.

If you are involved in a competitive situation, placing a painting with the tribute horse as the subject is one of the best ways of using symbolic Feng Shui to bring you victory luck. The horse signifies triumph over your competitors. If you cannot find such a painting, look for something that shows a horse (preferably white) that is laden with precious things and that is being led (not ridden) by an official. This symbolizes upward mobility and promotion. It is very auspicious indeed.

PLACE A PAIR OF JADE HORSES IN THE SOUTH OF THE LIVING ROOM FOR RECOGNITION LUCK.

The horse is favorably regarded as one of the precious animals that emits a great deal of Yang energy. It is also one of the precious animals included in the mandala offering to Buddha. It is emblematic of nobility, class, and a comfortable lifestyle. It stands for speed and perseverance. The horse should always be placed south in your house, and this means the south wall or corner of any of the rooms. It is best placed in the living and family areas and never in the bedrooms.

Do not display a horse that is rearing up and do not place such a rearing horse directly behind you or directly confronting you. You will suffer accidents and physical problems related to your limbs if you do that. Instead, let the horse be placed in a nonthreatening posture. Some wonderful replicas of auspicious horses are the famous Ming horse sculptures, which are ideal for the south part of your living room.

A PAIR OF PRECIOUS ELEPHANTS

The word for elephant in Chinese sounds like *hsiang*, which can also mean Prime Minister. The elephant is thus the symbol of strength, prudence, energy, and sound judgment – all the qualities of a good and moral leader. It is also one of the four animals that represent power (the other three being the tiger, the lion, and the leopard). The elephant is also regarded as one of the eight treasures of Buddhism, and it features strongly as one of the precious animals that is significantly included in the mandala offering made to Buddhist deities at pujas (*see* pages 116–121).

In Thailand, the white elephant is regarded as a holy creature, and in many Eastern cultures, deities and gods are often depicted riding atop an elephant. In Chinese culture, pictures of children seated on elephants are said to represent good fortune.

The Feng Shui significance of the elephant is that it brings plenty of good fortune associated with the rise of the patriarch to power and prominence. This is because the elephant is believed to be the bearer of the wish-granting jewel, so its symbolic presence in the home signifies the luck of having all your aspirations granted. The ideal way of displaying the elephant in the home is to buy a pair of ceramic elephants and place them either inside or outside the house, and on either side of the main entrance door. I prefer them inside my house to symbolize the arrival of good luck.

The elephant is also said to be an excellent symbol for granting descendants' luck to households. It is believed that childless women who have the image of an elephant in the bedroom will enhance their chances of getting a male child (*see also* page 120 for more on the precious elephant).

A PAIR OF PRECIOUS ELEPHANTS BRING GOOD FORTUNE AND DESCENDANTS' LUCK.

THE RED BAT

The red bat has been an auspicious emblem of prosperity, happiness, and longevity for a very long time and is the Yang symbol of good fortune. The origin of this positive connotation of what could well have been an obnoxious creature comes from the sound of its name. In Chinese, it is known as the *pian fu* and the word *fu* also sounds like happiness and good fortune. As such, the bat is a very popular symbol that is frequently used for decorative purposes. When utilized for Feng Shui, the bat is usually painted in a cinnabar red because red is also the color of joy. Usually, red bats are drawn in a cluster of five, the pictorial representation of the five blessings from heaven – old age or longevity, wealth, health, love of virtue, and a natural death. Five red bats also represent the Yang symbol of prosperity. These are usually drawn onto ceramics and paintings, and one of the more auspicious representations is of five bats emerging from a jar or vase. This means not only happiness and good fortune but also a peaceful life with few problems.

The Chinese believe that if a family of bats takes up residence in your home, it is an exceptionally good omen. It signifies the coming of a time of prosperity and success for the household. Thus bats should never be chased away. Last year a family of bats took up residence in the home of a friend of mine. Instead of chasing them away, I urged him to make the bats welcome. Since then his tour operator business has prospered by leaps and bounds.

THE GEM-SPOUTING MONGOOSE

The Chinese preoccupation with harnessing prosperity luck and overcoming bad luck is so pronounced that there are many other animals that symbolize getting wealth and overcoming bad luck. Some of these animals are easy to identify but others can be a bit tricky. I would like to introduce you to two symbols that you can place on your desk as a wealth energizer and to help overcome bad Feng Shui. The mongoose, for example, is said to spout precious gems and jewels from its mouth. He is featured as the principal wealth creator carried by all three of the Tibetan Buddhas of Wealth, the White Jambhala, the Yellow Jambhala, and the Black Jambhala. Followers of Tibetan Buddhism often display this Buddha of Wealth sitting under a fountain of water since this is believed to please him and will cause a mongoose to spout forth plenty of valuable gemstones and jewels.

The *pik yao* and *pik chen* are earth and sea variations of a particularly powerful creature that can overcome misfortune. He is said to have the power to assist anyone suffering from bad Feng Shui as a result of having offended the Grand Duke Jupiter. Thus those enduring a period of bad luck soon after moving into a new home or soon after undertaking renovations should display the image of the *pik yao* or *pik chen* in the home.

THE MONGOOSE IS ASSOCIATED WITH THE TIBETAN GOD OF WEALTH.

THE WISH-FULFILLING COW

Like the elephant in Thailand, the cow holds a special place in the hearts of the people of India. In Feng Shui, reference is made to the wish-fulfilling cow, which is said to be emblematic of good descendants' luck. In Buddhism and Hinduism the cow is regarded as a holy animal. For good luck, display the cow sitting on a bed of coins and ingots anywhere on your desk (*see also* page 107).

Other Symbols of Wealth

There are many symbolic representations of wealth that can be displayed to create prosperity luck within households. In the old days, all Imperial court households had a wide variety of such emblems, and today modern-day homes of Chinese tycoons continue to be lavishly decorated with often very expensive good fortune symbols.

PROTECTING THE FAMILY RICE SUPPLY

If your staple food is rice, always take care of the family rice urn. It does not matter how you keep your rice, and in what sort of container, but here are some useful ways to ensure that your symbolic rice bowl is always protected, thereby ensuring that your family's wealth and assets are never lost or squandered away.

- Always keep the rice urn closed. In addition to keeping rats and cockroaches out, this also signifies that your family wealth is protected.
- Do not use a plastic container to store your rice. Instead, use something that is made of ceramic or clay. The earth energy is sound and solid.
- Do not allow water to seep or drip into the rice urn. This makes the rice go bad and is not a good sign for the household.
- Place a red packet or envelope with real money inside your rice urn, at the very bottom. Or trace symbols of gold ornaments onto red paper and put them in your urn. Always top up with a fresh red packet at the start of each lunar New Year – this symbolizes that your family fortunes can only increase and expand.
- There is nothing so inauspicious as a rice urn that is allowed to get empty. Thus it is a good idea to replenish it as soon as the urn is half full.

- Do not allow anyone to empty the family rice urn, since this is considered the worst kind of Feng Shui. In fact, the upsetting of a container of rice on the table or elsewhere is considered so unlucky that in the old days, servants careless enough to do this were thrown out of the home immediately.
- Keep the rice urn hidden away inside a pantry, storeroom, or cupboard. This will ensure that you do not lose your wealth.
- There are no hard and fast rules regarding the shape of the rice urn but a deep urn is better than a shallow one. When the urn is deep it signifies that you have deep pockets with lots of money. If the rice bowl is shallow it suggests that you could run short of money.

CLUSTERS OF CRYSTALS

Energize your living rooms with beautiful crystals fashioned into wealth chests filled with fake precious jewels. They look very beautiful and also bring in plenty of Yang energy. Crystals are a great medium for Feng Shui symbolism because they represent earth energy.

If you wish, you can also display a cluster of natural quartz crystal. Place this kind of crystal energizer in the northwest or west to activate the gold energy of these two sectors.

THE MONEY TREE

There is an old Chinese legend that refers to a money tree that has branches of coins and gold. When you shake the money tree, gold coins fall like rain as if from heaven into your garden. This rainfall of coins and gold has become a popular motif in old paintings and screens, and needless to say has become a great favorite with enthusiasts who believe in the power of symbolic Feng Shui.

You can make a money tree in your yard by using lots of old coins. Use your creativity to create such a tree, paying close attention to the tying of coins to hang auspiciously down the tree. Note that the hanging coins are tied together with red thread. Among the branches add a dragon to add further symbolism, and on the stem write auspicious Chinese characters and inscriptions. Finally, at the base of the tree position three red lanterns, which serve to energize it. During the lunar New Year, red lanterns hung from the money tree signify wealth all year round. A variation of the money tree is the wish-fulfilling gem tree. These gem trees are extremely auspicious since they create wonderful lucky energy for the whole house (*see* page 106).

GOLDEN CHOPSTICKS

One of the best gifts to give someone is a pair of golden chopsticks although this is one of the lesser known good fortune symbols. I was so thrilled at the start of this year when I was presented with two pairs of chopsticks with matching horseshoe chopstick holders. One pair was gold and the other pair was silver. I consider this an extremely auspicious gift and am currently displaying them quite ostentatiously in my dining room for good luck. The chopstick symbolizes additional sources of income.

THE LAUGHING BUDDHA

The Laughing Buddha is one of the most beloved of Buddha images and can be seen in Chinese homes and Chinese restaurants throughout the world. He has been referred to as the Buddha of Wealth because his image is believed to bring prosperity and wealth luck to those engaged in any kind of business. Those who consider him the Buddha of Wealth assume that his big bag contains lots of gold ingots and precious gemstones. Some also maintain that all his wealth is carried in his round tummy, and that the bigger the tummy, the more auspicious the image. To enjoy the Buddha's blessings, they say, you should stroke the big belly each day.

Others say, however, that the Laughing Buddha is the Buddha of Happiness because he is said to love scooping up all the unhappiness, problems, and worries of human beings and stuffing them inside his big bag. Nothing makes him happier than transforming problems into happiness. And because all of humankind has so many problems his bag is said to be big and heavy. This is also the reason he is shown laughing happily – he is able to pick up what he loves most – other people's problems and unhappiness.

Place this Buddha in the living room, preferably directly facing the front door. Select any posture you wish. The Laughing Buddha is sculptured into many forms in many materials – perhaps look for a medium that corresponds to your most auspicious element.

THE LAUGHING BUDDHA IS ALSO THE BUDDHA OF ABUNDANT HAPPINESS. SHOWN HERE IS A SIGNATURE PIECE FROM THE AUTHOR'S COLLECTION.

2

SYMBOLS OF LONGEVITY

The Chinese believe that there is no good luck without long life, and that good Feng Shui creates longevity for the family patriarch and matriarch. Enhance the longevity and life span of all members of your household by displaying symbols of longevity in the home, and magnify their effect by placing them in the best Feng Shui orientation. Longevity means not only a healthy life but also one that is protected from fatal and life-threatening accidents and mishaps. To the Chinese, longevity is one of three significant aspirations. Every prayer and every salutation includes the wish for long life.

Gods and Immortals

Good Feng Shui can be enhanced by ceramic, wooden, and cloisonné figurines of various auspicious deities. These are traditional gods from legendary stories and Taoist beliefs. The deities featured here are extremely popular, and I recommend them for the symbolism of auspiciousness and happiness they each represent.

THE GOD OF LONGEVITY

Sau, the God of Longevity, is probably one of the most popular deities found in many Chinese homes (*see* the statue below) and he is usually depicted in paintings, drawn on porcelain and ceramics, and is also carved in wood, ivory, and stone. He is popular because he symbolizes good health and a smooth and long life. He is usually dressed in a yellow robe and carries a staff with the magical gourd tied to the top. The gourd itself is an auspicious symbol that, when carried by the God of Longevity, is said to be filled with the nectar of immortality.

Sau carries a peach, which is the fruit of immortality, and sometimes a crane and a deer also accompany him. At other times Sau is drawn with a pine tree, surrounded by longevity mushrooms known as *ling chi*. The mushrooms are often referred to by the Chinese as the plants of long life.

A STATUE OF SAU HOLDING A PEACH AND CARRYING HIS STAFF WITH THE MAGICAL GOURD.

Place Sau in a high place in full view of the entrance into the room where he is located. Place him with a solid wall behind. It is considered bad luck to have a window, a toilet, or the kitchen directly behind or directly in front of him. Instead, the best place for Sau is situated on a table placed in the corner that is diagonally opposite the door.

The God of Longevity is not a Buddhist deity. He is not worshiped in the same way that Buddha is worshiped, so do not place Sau on your altar since doing so does not make him more auspicious in any way. There is no necessity to treat Sau as a god in the Western sense. But it is also unlucky to place him on a table that is too low, so a coffee table is not a suitable place for him. When he is placed too low there is an implied lack of respect for what he stands for. The rule is that all symbolic deities placed in the home should ideally be at eye level with the residents of the household. If you have Sau as part of the three Star Gods in your home (*see* opposite) make sure that when the gods are facing you, Sau is placed on the right (their left).

Together, the three Star Gods are said to symbolize health, wealth, and happiness, interpreted as longevity, prosperity, and authority. They should be placed on a high side table in the dining room from where they are said to create auspicious Chi for the entire household. At the office, Fuk Luk Sau can be placed behind you, giving vital support and good fortune.

THE EIGHT IMMORTALS

The Eight Immortals are superior beings of Taoist legend. Comprising six men and two women, these beings are said to have lived at various times. They each attained immortality under different circumstances but legend says they have all tasted the nectar and peach of immortality.

The Eight Immortals are widely regarded as symbols of longevity and good fortune by Taoists. They are frequently depicted on Chinese porcelain vases and urns, each symbolizing their good fortune attributes. They are also drawn onto plates, usually as a group of eight crossing the waters or singly, wielding their respective symbols. They are also depicted in ivory, wood, and bronze, both as statues and decorative pieces. Students of the Chinese traditions sometimes compare them to the Buddhist Eighteen Arhats – enlightened beings said to have brought Buddhism to China and each also holding a personal symbol.

The Eight Beings (Hseen) and the Eighteen Arhats (Loharn) are said to possess supernatural powers and are capable of performing magic. Their symbolic presence in homes, on paintings or as statues in any medium, are believed to bestow good health, happiness, and general good fortune on families. It is for this reason that they are such popular subjects for artists and craftsmen. If you display them singly in your home it is useful to understand what they each signify.

- The chief of the Eight Immortals is Chung-Li Chuan who is generally shown as being fat and with a bare belly and holding a fan, which he uses to revive sick people. He is said to symbolize good health and to possess curative powers. Displayed in the home, he is said to cause residents to enjoy good health and live a healthy and long life.

THE THREE STAR GODS

Much Taoist literature refers to the seven stars that make up the Plow of the Great Bear constellation in the northern skies. Each of these stars is said to represent a heavenly deity and one aspect of good fortune. Of the seven, three star deities stand out prominently in the pantheon of good fortune symbols. These deities represent the three most important manifestations of good fortune, and they are collectively referred to as Fuk Luk Sau.

The First Star Deity reflects the universal wish for wealth and enhanced income. The God of Income and Prosperity (Fuk), wearing a red robe of a merchant and carrying a child, represents this: he sits on the right.

The Second Star Deity is the God of Authority (Luk). He represents the authority of the high government official and he holds the *ru yi* or scepter of office, in his left hand. The God of Authority always stands in the center.

The Third Star Deity reflects the universal wish for long life and this is represented by the God of Longevity (Sau) carrying a staff with a bottle gourd of nectar. He is usually accompanied by a white crane amid some pine branches and always sits on the left.

WATCHPOINT

Each of the Eight Immortals represents some special life circumstance and each holds a symbol that expresses a significant ability or power.

- The second immortal is Kuo-Lao Chang who carries a musical instrument shaped as a bamboo tube. He is said to possess the wisdom of the ages and has the ability to make himself invisible. This immortal is regarded as a sage whose image bestows wisdom on the family patriarch.
- The third immortal is Dong-Pin Lu, a scholar recluse regarded as the patron saint of the sick. He is said to have learned much of his magic craft from the chief of the immortals. On his back is a sword that he uses to overcome evil spirits and slice through sufferings caused by bad Chi energies. In his right hand is a fly swat, which he uses to cure illnesses. Displayed in the home, this immortal protects against illness caused by evil spirits and bad Chi.
- The fourth immortal is Guo-Chiu Tsao, who is reputed to have been related to an empress of the Sung Dynasty. He signifies nobility and is thus depicted in official robes. His symbol is a pair of castanets, held high up in his left hand. These symbolize his noble birth. Tsao is said to bestow recognition and attract high office for the family patriarch. Politicians and those wishing a life of power should invite his image into the home.
- The fifth immortal is Tieh-Guai Li, who looks like a beggar but is reputed to be the master of supernatural ability.
- The sixth immortal is Hsian-Tzu Han, who makes sweet sounds with his flute. This attracts good fortune Chi around him so all animals, insects, and plants thrive profusely in his presence. Han's special ability is to make plants bloom instantly. He keeps a profusion of plants in the sack he carries on his back.
- The seventh immortal is the woman in blue named Tsai-Ho Lan. She carries a flower basket and is said to epitomize the spirit of femininity.
- The eighth immortal is another woman, a fairy named Hsien Ku Ho. Her emblem is the holy lotus and the fly swat. Her presence in the home benefits the matriarch.

Symbolic Feng Shui borrows from Taoist legends, and the Eight Immortals symbolize the pinnacle of life aspirations. Place images of the immortals in your home either collectively in a painting or individually according to the desired effect. Each immortal is also said to signify one of the directions so should be placed accordingly to energize that direction.

THE BENEFITS OF THE EIGHT IMMORTALS

No	Name of immortal	Direction	Element	Symbol	Special benefit
1	Chung Li Chuan	east	wood	fan	Longevity and ceaseless energy
2	Kuo-Lao Chang	north	water	bamboo tube	Childless couples: put in bedrooms to conceive children
3	Dong-Pin Lu	northwest	gold	sword and fly swat	Cures illnesses; good scholar luck
4	Guo-Chiu Tsao	northeast	earth	castanets	Bestows luck for those who want power
5	Tieh-Guai Li	south	fire	bottle gourd	Bestows wisdom. Most powerful of the eight
6	Hsian-Tzu Han	southeast	wood	flute	Healing energies
7	Tsai-Ho Lan	west	gold	flower basket	Brings luck to young women
8	Hsien Ku Ho	southwest	earth	lotus	Family and marriage luck

THE QUEEN OF THE WEST

The Queen of the West is known as Hsi Wang Mu. She is often depicted with a retinue of five fairy attendants, seated on a peacock or phoenix, and wearing an elaborate headdress. She has a crane and other types of birds alongside. Doves serve as her messengers. She has two main attendants: one carries a bowl of the peaches of immortality and the other carries a large fan. The Queen of the West lives in a palace with extensive gardens in the holy Kun Lun mountains. In her manicured grounds there grow many different kinds of magical plants, including the fabled fairy peach plants that blossom, bear fruit, and ripen once every 3,000 years. Anyone eating these peaches will be made immortal.

The Queen of the West is a very popular subject of paintings and screens, and her images are often accompanied with brilliantly written good fortune verses that are said to bring extreme good luck to households.

THE EIGHT IMMORTALS ARE SUPERIOR BEINGS OF TAOIST LEGEND; THEY SYMBOLIZE THE TAOIST PINNACLE OF LIFE ASPIRATIONS – THE ATTAINMENT OF IMMORTALITY.

For 15 years I displayed a relatively old Hsi Wang Mu screen in my home, and each time I entertained a Feng Shui master to lunch he would comment extremely favorably on the screen and offer an interpretation of the auspicious Chinese characters that adorned it. Later, I presented the screen as a marriage gift to the son of a good friend.

The Queen of the West symbolizes many good things, including a long life filled with great honor, wealth, fame, and recognition. She brings obedient sons into households. Families stay together and siblings enjoy relationships that are free of petty squabbling. She is best shown with her attendants, seated on a carriage drawn by phoenixes and peacocks. Screens that feature her are easy to find in Hong Kong, Taiwan, and China and are best placed near the main front door.

Animate and Inanimate Symbols

To enjoy good health and a smooth ride through life, display the beautiful crane, the evergreen pine tree, or the succulent fruit of longevity – the peach. Grow a patch of bamboo or create a tortoise pond to capture the essence of this celestial creature's many auspicious qualities. Display a jade cicada to signify the good life in the afterlife.

THE BEAUTIFUL CRANE

The crane has a reputation of being the patriarch of all the feathered creatures of the earth. Next to the phoenix (see page 40), he is the most favored of all the bird symbols of good fortune. He is the bird of immortality and is strongly identified with the attributes of long life, happiness, and a smoothness of flight. His symbolic presence in the home or garden is believed to bring harmony and happiness to the home. It was these attributes that prompted me to display flowerpots with crane and pine tree designs, and to search for a marble crane sculpture to place in the south sector of my garden. I regard my cranes with great fondness and am convinced they bring me a great many opportunities as well as a smooth and happy life. There are four types of cranes in Chinese mythology: black, white, yellow, and blue. Of the four, the black crane is reputed to live the longest. He is said to live for 600 years.

The use of cranes as symbols of good fortune, and particularly as symbols of longevity, goes back to the time of the legendary Emperor Fu Hsi. Stories of the adventures of the Eight Immortals are peppered with references to the white crane. Drawn onto Chinese art

A PAIR OF WHITE CRANES IN THE HOME CREATES FAMILY HARMONY.

and craft objects, the crane is shown in many different poses, each of which convey subtle shades of meanings of good fortune, a few of which are given here:

• Shown flying and soaring to heaven, the crane symbolizes a good afterlife since it is often viewed as the conveyor of souls to heaven. For this reason, some people consider it auspicious to place a crane with outspread wings and uplifted foot in the center of a coffin during a funeral procession. This was believed to guide the soul safely to heaven.

• Shown among clouds, the crane symbolizes longevity, wisdom, and a life close to the emperor. Thus it signifies someone reaching a high position of power.

• Shown frolicking among pine trees, a crane denotes staying power, resilience, and a life filled with honors and wealth.

• Shown as a pair, cranes signify the long life of the family patriarch and matriarch. One of the best anniversary gifts to present to your beloved parents is artwork that shows a pair of beautiful white cranes nestling between branches of a pine tree. This denotes continuation of the family

PLACE A CRANE IN YOUR GARDEN
TO BRING HARMONY AND HAPPINESS
TO THE HOME. THE CRANE ALSO
SIGNIFIES LONGEVITY.

west, the crane brings good luck for the children, and placed in the north-west it favors the family patriarch. Placed in the east, the crane benefits the sons of the family, especially the eldest.

The sectors that do not benefit in any way from the crane's presence are kitchens, bathrooms, and toilets. It is perfectly acceptable to display cranes in bedrooms, dining rooms, and family rooms.

Screens that have cranes drawn on them make excellent Feng Shui cures for when there are three or more doors placed in a straight line in the house. Similarly, a screen like this is good if you wish to block out unlucky sights.

unit intact with both the patriarch and the matriarch. The real meaning, however, goes deeper. A pair of cranes also signifies the continuation of all the best qualities of the chien and kun trigrams as well as the protection of family harmony and well-being.

White cranes (those with the tuft of red on the head) are believed to bring harmony to households, ensuring that relationships within the family are harmonious. Cranes also signify wisdom, the kind that solves problems and dissolves obstacles that stand in the way of the family's upward progression.

The flying crane signifies attainment of great heights with honor, while a single white crane gazing upward at the sun or moon signifies aspiring to the ultimate wisdom. For a great number of reasons the white crane is a desirable symbol to display in the home.

The best corner of the home for the crane is the south since this brings opportunities. Placed in the

THE PINE TREE

The pine tree is probably the strongest symbol of inner strength and permanence. In the cold winter months, the pine does not lose its needles, thereby manifesting its steadfastness, strength, and fortitude. As a result, the pine is a favorite symbol of longevity and is probably the most frequently painted tree. Almost all landscape paintings show the pine with rocks and narcissus, which indicate a life of long-lasting personal achievements. Alternatively, when painted with the bamboo and the plum tree, the three friends in winter are represented. Painted together they signify friendship in adversity and through thick and thin.

ALWAYS RESPECT ANY
PINE TREES ON YOUR
PROPERTY; MAKE SURE
THEY STAY HEALTHY.

The pine tree is a popular subject of poetry. In the works of Confucius there are many references to the pine – most of the time used as a metaphor to illustrate its attributes of steadfastness and survival under particularly difficult conditions. Old pine trees are regarded with the greatest respect, so if you have grown pines on your property do treat them with respect. A pair of healthy pine trees in the yard is also a symbol of married bliss.

THE PEACH TREE

No other tree or fruit has greater depth of symbolic meaning than the peach tree. Every part of this plant is believed to possess some valuable attribute. Peach wood is said to be wonderful protection against naughty spirits and demons. Thus in the old days, weapons such as bows and arrows would be made of peach wood. Taoist priests also used peach wood to make their seals with which to signet their amulets and talismans with protective luck.

At the same time, peach blooms and petals are said to possess the power to cast romantic spells over men. Taoist magic love spells are said to require the use of the peach blossom to be effective. Sad to say I do not have the formula for making these love potions.

It is, however, the peach fruit that is said to be most valuable. Legend has it that the peach plant of immortality stood somewhere

THE FRUIT OF THE PEACH TREE
IS REGARDED AS HAVING
QUALITIES OF IMMORTALITY.

in the holy Kun Lun mountains of China in the fabled gardens of the Goddess of the West, Hsi Wang Mu. This miraculous tree was said to bear the peach fruit of immortality only once every 3,000 years, and once when it did, the Goddess invited the Eight Immortals to her garden for a feast. This was how they attained the status of immortality. Alas, just as the party got underway along came the Monkey God (together with a retinue of others) who harvested all the peaches and attained immortality. Thus, placing the image of the Monkey God stealing the peaches of immortality in your home is said to endow it with a great deal of longevity energies. I have just such a wood sculpture in my home. I bought it many years ago in Fukien province in China and was told this beautiful legend that lay behind the symbolic meaning of the sculpture.

The peach is also the symbol of spring, for it is during this time that the peach tree blooms in China. Spring is said to be the best time for couples to get married, and the peach is also a symbol of marriage. Placing a picture of peaches in your bedroom is believed to create the Chi of marriage thereby enhancing marriage opportunities for single men and women of the family. Get a jadeite peach plant with five peaches from a Chinese arts and crafts shop.

THE BAMBOO

The bamboo has long been regarded as a symbol of longevity primarily because of its durability. Biologically it is regarded as a kind of grass and yet it can grow taller than many trees. Bamboo thrives on almost any kind of soil, and it is continuously green despite weather conditions. It endures through the coldest of winters and the hottest of summers. When the wind blows it bends with the flow, sometimes bending as low as the ground itself. This signifies the way difficulties should be faced. The bamboo bends, adapts, goes with the flow, but it never changes. And after the storm it always survives. In China, the bamboo

plant grows throughout the country, as far north as Beijing. There are about ten species of bamboo and within each species, there are many different varieties. All varieties of the bamboo can be displayed to actualize the Chi of longevity.

There are different legends associated with each variety of bamboo. Thus the spotted bamboo signifies undying love and fidelity since it is said to be the tears of the emperor's consorts. The spiny bamboo has more leaves than stems and this variety signifies the luck of old age associated with good family luck. The patriarch will have the good fortune to enjoy the successes of the descendants. The solid stemmed bamboo signifies a life that is free of illness and disease. Good health is associated with these sturdy versions of the bamboo plant.

In the old days, the growing of bamboo groves epitomized the symbolic presence of the longevity Chi. Those wanting to manifest the bamboo plant Chi can do so by placing potted bamboo plants near the front part of the home, or along the east side of the garden. This is the sector of the wood element and is good for placing the auspicious bamboo.

It is a good idea to hang classical paintings of the leafy bamboo in the study or office to ensure longevity of good fortune associated with work and career. Select paintings that show groups of dangling bamboo leaves in numbers that are auspicious. In this connection, groups of six, seven, eight, and nine leaves (or multiples thereof) are deemed to be auspicious, while groups of two, three, and five leaves are deemed to be less auspicious. The best combinations are bamboo leaves in groups of six and eight.

The bamboo is also a symbol of endurance and protection. In winter, many homes in China would have groves of bamboo plants that act as shields against the cold north winds. Thus bamboo grown in the north part of the garden symbolizes protection. If your home suffers from cold winds and requires protection during the winter months plant a curtain of bamboo where it most effectively shelters you, irrespective of the direction.

THE DEER

The deer is a very popular symbol associated with speed, endurance, and long life. In the Yangtze valley, the deer resembles the antelope, and in the south-western mountains of China in the mountains bordering on Tibet, it looks like the yak.

Phonetically, the deer in Chinese sounds like the word *lu*, which also means good income and prosperity. As such, the deer also signifies wealth. Together with its other meaning, the deer thus means a long life filled with wealth and prosperity. It is therefore extremely auspicious to have the image of the deer in the office of businessmen and -women. Displayed in the work place, the deer symbolizes the wish for the company to prosper and grow. Displayed at home – and especially if standing on a bed of coins or gold ingots – it means the family living there will enjoy a long life of ease and growing prosperity.

THE CHINESE WORD FOR DEER IS *LU*, MEANING INCOME, SO THIS
ANIMAL IS REGARDED AS A SYMBOL OF WEALTH AS WELL AS LONGEVITY.

There are many folk legends associated with the deer in central and north Asia but in Chinese mythology it is almost always shown accompanying Sau, the God of Longevity. Many Chinese artists also like to depict the deer next to a high court official since this represents the wish that the recipient will achieve fame, riches, and a long career. This makes it an excellent gift for someone who wishes to advance in his or her career, or for someone who has just graduated and is embarking on a working career.

THE JADE CICADA

To the Chinese, the cicada is a most powerful emblem of immortality, and in the old days rich families would often bury their dead with a piece of jade carved in the form of a cicada in the corpse's mouth. It was believed that this would immortalize the ancestor, giving him or her a good life after death.

For the living, the cicada was regarded as a symbol of long life, happiness, and eternal youth. This was probably due to the fact that the cicada is the longest living insect. Some say it lives for as long as 18 years. The origin of this symbolism can also be attributed to the legend of the cicada being in reality a queen in ancient times who did many good deeds during her reign. On her death the queen was believed to have been reborn as a cicada. As a cicada she never grew old physically and she lived longer than all other insects. Since then, the cicada has been regarded as a symbol of a youthful appearance.

Corporate players in the modern business environment requiring protection against jealous colleagues or scheming bosses might find it useful to search for a jade cicada to wear as a pendant amulet around the neck. Failing this, look for a cicada paperweight and place it on your desk in the office. Naturally, if you cannot afford a cicada made from jade look for one made of a material that simulates and looks like the translucent jade.

The Chinese have always valued calligraphy, which is the art of skilfully painting characters with the Chinese brush such that the strength, the stamina, and the intrinsic Chi (or special life force energy) is successfully transferred onto paper. From a Feng Shui perspective, calligraphy represents the end result of good human Chi in action, and this harmonizes with the Chi of the environment to bring about good fortune. Calligraphy is thus considered a manifestation of good Feng Shui. When the characters that are written are also auspicious words, or words that connote different types of good fortune, it is even more auspicious. Thus hanging stylish calligraphy is usually regarded as good Feng Shui.

A popular word frequently rendered in calligraphy is that which means longevity. The word for longevity is "sau." Two versions of this word are illustrated below. Learn to recognize this word and look for it in Chinese art, costume, and decorative symbols. It is good to hang such calligraphy in the bedroom of the patriarch.

THE TORTOISE

I have found that nothing beats the tortoise as a symbol of longevity in the home. But bear in mind that it does have a multidimensional meaning and although having its presence in the home is said to ensure that family patriarchs live to well beyond 80 years of age, it is also a symbol of protection, support, wealth, and prosperity. The tortoise is also the only celestial creature that actually exists – and it (or a terrapin or turtle) is easy to find. In Feng Shui, the tortoise signifies the protective hills of the north as well as the back support that ensures the luck of a home stays firm, strong, and auspicious.

The tortoise is also said to conceal within its body and within the design motifs on its shell all the secrets of heaven and earth. I started writing books about Feng Shui soon after I picked up the shell of a dead turtle washed up on the shore on a seaside vacation trip to Pangkor Island with my family. That was in 1992. At that time I failed to note the significance of that omen, and although I brought the shell back home, I discarded it soon afterward. I only realized the symbolism while one day meditating by my pond where my pet terrapins live (terrapins are freshwater or tidewater turtles; the land species are usually referred to as tortoises).

THE BEST WAY TO DISPLAY A DRAGON TORTOISE IS ON A BED OF COINS WITH A COIN IN ITS MOUTH.

Of course, my story pales into inconsequence next to the many legends of the tortoise that describe its mystical and enigmatic symbolism. A magical tortoise was said to have helped the Emperor Fu Hsi to tame the raging Yellow River (the Hwang Ho). It is also believed that when Pan Ku created the world he used tortoises as pillars to hold up the universe. The tortoise's humped back was the sky, its belly was the earth, and its legendary longevity made it indestructible. Even better would be a display of the dragon tortoise on a bed of coins, symbolizing longevity and wealth.

THE GOURD

The bottle gourd is both a Taoist and Buddhist symbol of longevity and good fortune. It is a powerful tool of Taoist magic and at the same time is also considered a receptacle of the holy nectar of many Buddhist deities. It is featured in many old paintings of both traditions. Thus the God of Longevity carries a staff at the end of which is a bottle gourd said to contain the elixir of immortality (*see* page 50).

Displaying a dried gourd in and around the home is a good omen. It suggests that the home receives many blessings and is visited by these holy beings. It is probably for this reason also that many temples are decorated with many such bottle gourds. Merely wearing a small miniature of the gourd fashioned in gold around the neck is said to ward off pernicious influences and accidents since it is such a powerful longevity symbol.

A PAIR OF VASES SHAPED LIKE BOTTLE GOURDS ENDOWS A HOME WITH SPECIAL BLESSINGS AND A LONG LIFE FOR ITS OCCUPANTS.

3

SYMBOLS FOR
LOVE AND ROMANCE

By combining Chinese astrology with the Feng Shui of
the five elements, you can use potent symbols of romance
to jazz up your love life, enhance your friendships, get
an unwilling lover to commit, and energize the conjugal
happiness of your marriage. Discover the potency of love
symbols. Place a pair of mandarin ducks and watch them
bring love back into a sagging marriage. Hang or
display beautiful peonies to enhance romance in your
special relationships; and wear the double happiness
symbol for greater marriage joy.

Love Luck

I n Feng Shui, love and romance always means the luck of having a happy marriage and family life that is blessed with many bright, happy children. Thus all the love energizers bring marriage opportunities to unmarried single men and women, and they enhance the love, commitment, and loyalty between spouses.

Using symbols of conjugal happiness to activate romance luck implies a desire for permanent commitment. In the Chinese view of family there is no suggestion of frivolous relationships outside marriage. Marriages are regarded as sacred, and infidelity as we presently know it did not really exist.

However, olden Chinese society was polygamous. Men frequently had several wives and concubines. As such it is important to be careful when choosing and displaying love symbols. Don't overdo the presence of these love symbols in case they result in the men developing a roving eye. Also take note of some simple safeguards to ensure that an outside third party does not come between those in the relationship.

ACTIVATING FOR LOVE

Before marriage, activating for love brings marriage opportunities but it does not guarantee a permanent conjugal commitment between a couple. Thus Feng Shui can help attract marriage opportunities for men and women, but it cannot guarantee the quality of the mate. Also, it is useful to know that if the marriage corner happens to be occupied by a toilet, then displaying a love symbol inside the toilet room could well attract a most unsuitable match, one who could bring bad luck to the relationship. Do not do anything to activate the Chi inside the toilet.

Usually, the marriage and romance corner is the place of the matriarchal trigram kun, and this is the southwest sector of any home. Use a compass to determine the southwest. If the main door happens to be in the southwest or this corner of the home is occupied by a toilet or is missing, marriage opportunities of single residents are seriously afflicted. In this case, look for the southwest sector of the bedroom or living room to activate with love symbols.

After marriage, connubial bliss between the spouses depends on their heaven luck or karma. However, their

THE SOUTHWEST SECTOR CORRELATES WITH MARRIAGE AND ROMANCE. ACTIVATE THESE AREAS IN THE LIVING ROOM AND BEDROOM FOR GOOD MARRIAGE LUCK.

marriage karma can be greatly enhanced with a Feng Shui inspired display of symbols of family harmony. These should always include symbols that signify lots of sons since this is still presumed by some to be the main determinant of happiness. Indeed, many marriage and good fortune rituals associated with wedlock are connected to the wish for sons, and wealthy families frequently went to great lengths to ensure that the Feng Shui of the family mansion took this aspiration into account. Consequently, the selection of symbols in this section of the book includes those that magnify family harmony and those that ensure plenty of offspring.

MANDARIN DUCKS

Mandarin ducks are the famous symbols of lovers. Placed as a pair in any space, they create the kind of Chi that is most conducive for lovers to become a married couple. In fact, a pair of mandarin ducks is probably the most potent symbol of married bliss. Thus anyone wanting to energize his or her love life should go out and get an image of these ducks.

It would be best, however, to avoid ducks that are carved out of wood because this material clashes with the element that needs to be energized: that of earth. Small wood would not matter, but carved mandarin ducks are usually made of big wood element, i.e. wood from big trees. Because of this, I usually recommend to my single friends in search of love, either to display a painting of a pair of ducks or to find sculptures of mandarin ducks that are made of a semiprecious stone. This will magnify the earth element, which in turn

A POTENT SYMBOL OF MARRIED BLISS:
A PAIR OF MANDARIN DUCKS.

strongly activates the kun trigram of the southwest, the sector that signifies romance and marriage. So placing a pair of ducks in the southwest sector of your living room, your bedroom, or your home will activate love and marriage Chi.

Of the semiprecious stones used to make the ducks, the most potent would be red jasper, red cornelian, or red coral. Of the three, jasper is the least expensive and also the best. This is because the color of jasper is extremely favorable for the southwest corner. A second reason is that there are minute traces of iron in jasper and this makes the stone a very powerful energizer. In fact, the potency of most auspicious symbols is strongly magnified when fashioned out of jasper. This is especially the case for symbols that are said to be suitable for the earth corners of the home.

A PAIR OF GEESE

While the mandarin duck is said to symbolize conjugal fidelity, a pair of geese soaring high together signifies the happy togetherness of the married state. A pair of geese holds out the promise of a marriage being gloriously happy with no separation between the spouses. If you are newly married and work tends to keep you separated, look for a screen with a pair of flying geese or for images of two flying geese to hang on the southwest wall of your living room. They make for very happy relationships. These creatures have beautiful plumage and are said to pine for their mates. They are supposedly so attached to each other that one will never fly without the other.

Geese are also said to symbolize the male Yang energy so they are emblems of good fortune. In the winter they instinctively fly south toward the source of warmth. Being migratory birds, geese signify the spirit of adventure. But they never fly singly. They always fly in pairs, and as a marriage or betrothal gift they symbolize wishes of togetherness for the happy couple. Geese are faithful creatures. They do not mate a second time. Due to this attribute, the goose is also seen as a symbol of undying love. Those people who stay true to the memory of their departed loved ones are said to personify the spirit of the goose.

A PAIR OF GEESE REPRESENTS FIDELITY AND A LONG-LASTING MARRIAGE.

THE DOUBLE HAPPINESS SIGN

The Chinese have many symbols for signifying conjugal happiness but happiness Chi is most efficiently created by doubling the word happiness itself. Thus the most powerful and widely recognized symbol of marital happiness is the double happiness sign, shown below. This sign can be found carved on marital beds, chairs, and other bedroom furniture. It is also printed onto silks and brocades meant for wearing on the marriage day. In addition, invitation cards summoning guests to a wedding often have the double happiness sign prominently embossed into its design.

In a culture where superstition and social mores were scrupulously adhered to during the old days, the ritual of marriage was confined only to marriages contracted between a man and his first and principal wife. In the same way, therefore, the double happiness symbol could only be used to decorate and energize the wedding furniture and festivities of the man's first marriage. All subsequent marriages were deemed undeserving of the epitaph "double happiness." Fortunately, this nonsense does not hold any credence now.

Calligraphy featuring the double happiness character is also an excellent way of displaying the sign in the home. But only hang it in your bedroom in the sector that represents your personalized marriage corner based on the Eight Mansions or Kua Formula (*see* page 68). This will successfully create excellent marriage happiness Chi for you. I have used the double happiness symbol to decorate many pieces of my furniture, and I do it to create a harmonious flow of happy energy through my home.

THE MOUNTAIN PEONY

The peony is China's queen of flowers. It signifies beauty, romance, and the amorous feelings of youth. The peony comes in a variety of stunning colors, but it

USE THE DOUBLE HAPPINESS SIGN TO PROMOTE HAPPINESS CHI.

is the red peony that symbolizes love and is usually the color most admired and valued. If you hang a painting of red peonies in your home it signifies you have beautiful and eligible daughters whose hands in marriage are still available.

Displaying peonies in the living room always benefits the young daughters of a family because it is said to bring many suitors. The peony makes them witty and charming. Some say the legendary figure who is known as the White Peony was the pseudonym of a fairy creature so skilled in the arts of love she became a legend among those who pursued such pleasures.

Displaying peonies in the bedroom is an enticement for a sexual (and sometimes illicit) entanglement. So I always discourage married couples – especially those who have been married for a decade or more – from hanging a painting of the mountain peony in their bedroom. This will merely encourage the libido of the husband, causing him to look for "sweet young things" outside of the marriage.

Instead, always place a peony painting or vase of peonies in the living room. The motivation should be for it to benefit the daughters of the family and only those of marriageable age who are still living with the family. Once they marry and leave the family home, it is advisable to remove the peony painting.

THE FLITTING BUTTERFLY

The butterfly is a symbol of young love. This happy creature flits from flower to flower sipping sweet nectar from the blooms, signifying a happy social life for the youthful. It is the happiness of a frivolous sort, suggesting a period of a young person's life when it is not yet time for marriage. Some say therefore that the butterfly symbolizes love that is not serious.

Butterflies generally connote young men with a flirtatious nature and are suitable for those who want to create the Feng Shui of an active social life but who are not yet ready to make a commitment. Therefore this symbol is not very suitable for women since it suggests a situation where there is little romance and plenty of fun – a situation more traditionally suited, it would seem, to the male than the female.

A SINGLE PERSON SEEKING A LONG-TERM COMMITMENT SHOULD DISPLAY PEONIES IN THE LIVING ROOM.

According to legend, however, the butterfly signifies an undying bond between lovers. There is told the story of two young lovers, the man is a scholar, and the woman is the daughter of a rich magistrate. The lovers met, fell in love, and then were forced to separate by her parents. Heartbroken, the lovers die and in death are reunited. Reincarnated as butterflies, the two are together forever.

As a result of this famous legend of star-crossed lovers, there are those who maintain that butterflies symbolize eternal, rather than frivolous love. The romantics at heart would benefit hugely from placing the image of a pair of butterflies in the southwest corner of the home.

If you are one of those people who like butterflies and wish to display them in your home, remember that butterflies that have been preserved and are displayed "pinned" to a wooden board emit quite a lot of Yin energy. They represent death because they really are dead butterflies, which is not such a good idea to display as a symbol. Instead, it is far better to hang a picture of auspicious flowers with butterflies as part of the picture. This also introduces the concept of life, and the flying butterfly emits Yang rather than Yin energy.

PICTURES OF BUTTERFLIES FLITTING AMONG FLOWERS EMIT YANG ENERGY.

THE LUTE

Chinese string instruments (referred to as lutes) are believed to go as far back in history as to the time of Fu Hsi. Traditional lutes of ancient times are reputed to have been made of wood from the phoenix tree. Ritual soaking of the wood and taking the measurements often accompanied their production. Originally the lute had five strings, which emitted five notes, and this corresponded to the five elements. Later this was extended to seven strings. The word lute is used to describe 25 different string instruments and they are said to produce sounds so harmonious they signify the state of perfect union between a married couple. These sounds supposedly express not merely the sexual bliss of matrimony but more importantly also exemplify the friendship between the patriarch and the matriarch. Both purity and moderation are invoked by the sweet sounds, as a result of which the instruments have come to symbolize harmony and happiness in family life.

The lute is actually credited as having eight attributes, namely, happiness, elegance, sweetness, subtlety, nostalgia, softness, resonance, and strength. These are qualities that describe matrimonial and family happiness. Hang a painting of a woman playing this musical instrument and the vibrations created will be most beneficial.

TRADITIONAL CHINESE LUTES HAD FIVE STRINGS, REPRESENTING THE FIVE ELEMENTS. THE HARMONIOUS SOUNDS ARE EMBLEMATIC OF MATRIMONIAL HAPPINESS.

THE MAGPIE

The sacred magpie features strongly in old Manchu legends relating to its defeat of the Ming rulers and the founding of its dynastic rule over China. Thus, for many centuries the Manchus regarded it as a magical bird.

The literal translation of magpie is bird of joy and it is popularly believed that when the magpie nests in your house, it brings much cause for celebration and many happiness occasions. Those wishing to settle down will find the opportunity to do so. Those wanting love and marriage will find it, and those wishing

A MAGPIE IS A LUCKY BIRD THAT SYMBOLIZES LOVE AND MARRIAGE.

to have children will also be successful.

In addition to being a bringer of joy, the magpie is also considered to be a bird of good omen. If you were to fantasize on a plan to get rich, think through a strategy for getting a new job, or start a new venture, suddenly seeing a magpie is said to be a sign that you will succeed in attaining your goals. It is therefore a good idea to have either an image or a painting of a magpie in your home.

However, just because it is a bird of good omen, this does not mean you should keep the magpie in captivity. Do not keep any bird in captivity since this creates inauspicious Chi for the home and it is extremely unlucky since this symbolizes an inability to fly. The Chi will be afflicted and seriously limit your ability to grow, develop, and move upward in your career. Other lucky birds whose images are said to bring family harmony if displayed in the south sector of your home are the rooster, peacock, flamingo, mandarin duck, goose, and crane.

PAPER LANTERNS

There are many beautiful stories that describe the way lanterns cast auspicious light on humble abodes, enhancing the living space and bringing occasions of great joy to families. Lanterns written with auspicious characters or decorated with beautiful symbols have always been regarded as emblems of fertility. Thus to enhance the speedy conception of a child, lamps were often strategically placed under the bridal bed. Such lamps were named children and grandchildren lamps.

Sometimes, two red lanterns were hung on each side of the bridal bed, one for the bride and the other for the groom. These lamps were lit together and if they burned at the same rate, going out at the same time, it was regarded as an auspicious sign indicating a long and happy marriage. Such lanterns would often have the auspicious double happiness word printed on the lamp, and these came in various designs. The lanterns were believed to attract the precious Yang Chi that often caused conception leading to the birth of a son. When the wife became pregnant, the lamp continued to be lit each night.

THE GOD OF MARRIAGE

The Chinese God of Marriage is named Chieh Lin and he is none other than the old man on the moon. He is believed to be in charge of all nuptials between mortals, and reportedly sanctions unions between potential couples on earth by symbolically tying their feet together with an invisible red silk cord.

This belief inspired the custom of the bride and groom at Chinese weddings sealing their marriage pledge to each other by drinking wine from two glasses that are tied together with red cord. To activate romance luck in your home, therefore, it is an excellent idea to display a painting of the full moon. Such an image signifies Yang in Yin, and the fifteenth day of each month in the lunar calendar becomes a most auspicious time for undertaking all projects relating to matters of the heart.

Alternatively, use a lot of vermilion red in the southwest sector to jazz up the fire energy of this corner. As any Chinese person knows, red has always been the color of happiness and joy. Thus to energize romance and marriage luck, introduce drapes, wallpaper, and carpets that contain plenty of vermilion.

A PAPER LANTERN IS CONSIDERED A SYMBOL OF FERTILITY, ESPECIALLY WHEN DECORATED WITH AUSPICIOUS CHARACTERS.

ENERGIZE ROMANCE LUCK WITH RED WALLPAPER AND DRAPES IN THE SOUTHWEST SECTOR.

The vermilion red of fire produces earth in the productive cycle of element relationships, and this, together with the strong presence of Yang, should successfully activate the southwest. Do all this in the living room and not your bedroom, however. When there is too much Yang energy in the bedroom, you will find it difficult to have a good night's sleep.

If you prefer, it works equally well to install bright lights in the southwest of the living area. Lights also suggest Yang energy and they are excellent for activating the earth energy of the sector. Turn on the light for at least three hours each evening. In Feng Shui, fire energy is almost always a powerful energizer. But don't overdo it with too much light and remember that lights are not so good for the northwest and west sectors.

CRYSTALS FOR ROMANCE LUCK

By placing a crystal in the southwest corner, your bedroom will be excellent for activating romance, love, and marriage opportunities. Place it as near to the bed as possible.

You can also use quartz or amethyst crystals and, if you like, you can have them as smooth pebbles. If you place them with a growing plant, it is best that you put it in your living room and not the bedroom.

Smooth crystal balls are also wonderful energizers, and in fact are better than pebbles. They are excellent for relationship luck and for networking luck since they attract powerful people into your life. To activate this kind of luck, you should have six crystal balls. They do not all need to be the same size but they should ideally be in the northwest sector of the living room.

Love and the Kua Formula

In addition to energizing the southwest corner of your home and bedroom for romance and marriage luck, anyone wanting to improve a serious relationship (be it in a marriage or in any other kind of relationship) should learn about the Kua Formula. This is part of the Eight Mansions Compass Formula of Feng Shui and it is extremely powerful in activating different types of luck, including marriage and romance luck. First, you should learn how to determine your individual Kua number.

DETERMINING YOUR KUA NUMBER

Use the lunar calendar on pages 126–127 to determine your exact year of birth and then add together the last two digits. If you get two digits keep adding until you reduce them to one digit, e.g. if you get the number 10 then 1 + 0 = 1; or for number 14, 1 + 4 = 5. Then:

- For men, deduct this number from 10. The result is your Kua number.
- For women, add this number to 5. The result is your Kua number.

EXAMPLE 1

If you were born on August 28, 1957, then adding 5 + 7 = 12 and then adding 1 + 2 = 3.

- Then for men, 10 – 3 = 7, so the Kua is 7.
- For women it will be 3 + 5 = 8, so the Kua is 8.

EXAMPLE 2

If you were born on January 2, 1962, then because this date is before the lunar New Year you must deduct 1 from the year of birth. You must use 1961. So to calculate your Kua number you add together 6 + 1 = 7.

- Then for men, 10 – 7 = 3, so the Kua is 3.
- For women, 7 + 5 = 12 and then 1 + 2 = 3, so the Kua is also 3.

To energize your love mansion you should take note of where it is. Your love mansion is where your nien yen location is. For this check the table opposite.

ENERGIZE YOUR NIEN YEN CORNER OR LOVE MANSION

Different people should energize different corners of their homes to activate their respective love mansion location. This is in addition to the southwest location that enhances relationships luck for everyone. The southwest benefits everyone because it is the place of the kun trigram, which indicates the luck for love and romance as well as the luck of the family staying as a cohesive and happy unit.

Now you know which is your nien yen location you can set about energizing the correct corner of the living room. But don't stimulate the sector in your bedroom and don't overdo things. One energizing symbol is often enough to get the Chi flowing. Examples of ways to energize your nien yen sector according to your Kua number are given on pages 70–71.

Remember that symbols of love need not be Chinese. Anything that suggests love creates good Chi. It is a mistake to think that only Chinese symbols work. You can look for symbols of romance from

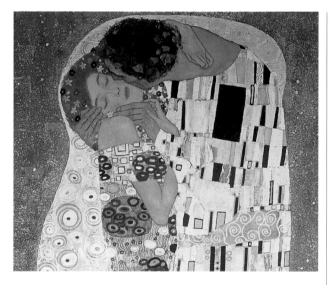

GUSTAV KLIMT'S "THE KISS" SUGGESTS INTENSE AND EXCITING ROMANCE.

your own personal culture and belief systems as well. Symbolism in Feng Shui has to do with the quality of energy, and the stronger the belief systems, the stronger will be the energies created. For this reason, I was not really surprised when my own Feng Shui expert, the wonderful Master Yap Cheng Hai, suggested red hearts and Western love birds in place of the double happiness and phoenix symbols when asked to energize the romance luck for someone's daughter.

Following this connection, some of the most powerful symbols of love would be the prints of romantic paintings. By this I do not mean sexually charged paintings but rather those that suggest either conjugal love or family happiness. Thus I have always loved Gustav Klimt's "The Kiss," a stunning painting with awesome power to suggest intense and exciting romance. When you come across any painting that seems to move you with its romanticism, do get it and

hang it in your home. Remember, different people find different things romantic.

Another powerful energizer of love Chi that was invented by the West is the crystal chandelier, which is also an excellent Feng Shui symbol because it signifies the Yang energy of earth come alive.

Remember that when you energize for love, you will be the most powerful enhancer of the energies of your space. Many people forget this is one of the things that makes symbolic Feng Shui work so well. The human psyche energizes strongly through its own belief systems. By understanding the basis of the symbolic meanings that lie behind objects, we empower the objects with positive accumulations of Chi energy. This, when applied with proper Feng Shui understanding of the five elements, attracts into our world wonderful happiness luck. So when you are energizing for romance luck do not be afraid to allow room for your own creativity to show through.

YOUR NIEN YEN LOCATION		
YOUR KUA NUMBER	YOUR NIEN YEN LOCATION	THE ELEMENTS TO ENERGIZE
1 east group	south	fire and wood
2 west group	northwest	metal and earth
3 east group	southeast	wood and water
4 east group	east	wood and water
5 west group	northwest for males	metal and earth
	west for females	metal and earth
6 west group	southwest	earth and fire
7 west group	northeast	earth and fire
8 west group	west	metal and earth
9 east group	north	water and metal

FOR PEOPLE WITH KUA 4, STIMULATE THE EAST SECTOR WITH A JADE DECORATIVE PIECE.

FOR PEOPLE WITH KUA 2, DISPLAY A WIND CHIME IN THE NORTHWEST SECTOR.

STIMULATING YOUR SECTOR

KUA NUMBER 1

Energize the south wall and corner of your home. The elements to activate are fire and wood. Here are three suggestions:

- Paint the south wall yellow, white, or red.
- Hang a red double happiness lantern.
- Place a pair of mandarin ducks or geese in the south corner. For opportunities to find love you can also display the celestial phoenix or a rooster. If you are a woman, display the male Yang phoenix, which is more colorful; and if you are a man, place a female Yin phoenix. Or place a dragon and phoenix together.

KUA NUMBER 2

Activate the northwest wall or corner of your home. The elements to magnify are metal and earth. Here are three suggestions:

- Hang a metal wind chime with six rods.
- Paint the northwest wall a metallic color.
- Have a brass or ceramic vase in the northwest corner.

KUA NUMBER 3

Activate the southeast corner or wall, and energize the elements wood and water. Some suggestions include the following:

- Place a deep and wide-brimmed bowl of water and grow a small green plant in this water. Keep the water clean and the plant healthy.
- Keep a pair of goldfish with bubbling oxygenators in a small aquarium.
- Display a big vase full of silk peonies – red or pink.

KUA NUMBER 4

Activate the east wall or corner of your home. Magnify the elements big wood and water. Some suggestions are as follows:

- Display a healthy flowering plant.
- Display the dragon image.
- Display a jade decorative piece.

FOR PEOPLE WITH KUA 3, ACTIVATE THE SOUTHEAST CORNER WITH A VASE OF SILK PEONIES.

KUA NUMBER 5

Activate the northwest corner or wall for men, and the west wall for women. Energize the elements metal and earth. Some suggestions include the following:

- Put up a six- or seven-rod wind chime.
- Place six crystal balls in the northwest and seven in the west.
- Display a moon symbol.

KUA NUMBER 6

Activate the southwest wall or corner of your home. Magnify the elements earth and fire. Some suggestions are as follows:

- Place a cluster of natural quartz crystal.
- Hang a small crystal chandelier.
- Display a lamp with a bright vermilion red lampshade.

KUA NUMBER 7

Activate the northeast wall or corner of your home. Magnify the elements earth and fire, and the suggestions would be similar to those for Kua number 6.

KUA NUMBER 8

Activate the west wall or corner of your home. Magnify the elements metal and earth, and the suggestions are similar to those for Kua number 5.

KUA NUMBER 9

Activate the north wall or corner of your home. Magnify the elements water and metal. Some suggestions are as follows:

- A brightly lit aquarium with many fast swimming fish (guppies or goldfish).
- A metal vase with auspicious designs.
- A painting of water scenery.

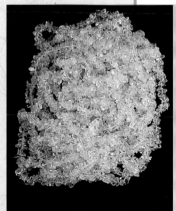

4

AUSPICIOUS RITUALS
FOR MARRIAGES
AND BIRTHDAYS

If you wish, you can observe good fortune rituals associated with marriage, birthdays, and other *hei see* or happy occasions that mark the turning points of a life. Many of these rituals verge on superstition and they incorporate Feng Shui symbols that add meaning and color to the celebratory occasions of life, Chinese style. These rituals (and taboos) reflect the rich symbolism of the Chinese tradition, underlying which is the desire to ensure that happy occasions are celebrated in a way that attracts a continuous flow of good fortune.

Horoscopes

Checking compatibility between couples highlights areas of potential conflict. In the old days, the Chinese deemed horoscope readings a sensible prerequisite of a marriage commitment. These days it is not a prerequisite but it is certainly a good idea to check horoscopes and, if necessary, use Feng Shui as an antidote to incompatibility.

CHECKING COMPATIBILITY FROM HOROSCOPES

The Chinese have a beautiful belief about couples being preordained from birth to marry each other. The story goes that the God of Marriage, the old man in the moon (*see* page 67), pairs off young girls and boys at birth by tying invisible red silk threads onto their toes. When they grow up and meet they will be powerfully drawn to each other and a marriage between them is the definite outcome. They will also be astrologically well suited to each other.

However, not all couples that are meant for each other in this way succeed in meeting. Sometimes invisible Chi forces create obstacles that stand in the way of their ever meeting. To overcome these obstacles, it is a good idea to use all the methods given in the previous chapter to activate and enhance marriage luck. Furthermore, to ensure that any impending match will be successful, casting a marriage horoscope would be an excellent idea. In the old days, marriages among the children of powerful and rich families were never left to chance since matchmakers would have worked closely with parents to arrange suitable matches. Suitability was based on the respective horoscopes of the couple. Marriage horoscopes were part of elaborate rituals performed prior to a marriage. In today's world, even if we have done away with the matchmaker, checking the horoscope surely cannot hurt.

OBTAINING A MARRIAGE HOROSCOPE

I strongly recommend that the Eight Character charts of a couple should be examined to ensure compatibility. These can be bought from websites that offer compatibility readings. Computerized programs make the calculations, so it easy to get these horoscope charts cast.

The charts basically reveal the weighting of the five elements and use the productive and destructive cycles of elements so that you can see immediately if two people are compatible. Even better is to go to a professional expert on the Four Pillars and Eight Characters. If you find all this too tedious, I suggest you at least undertake a reading based on the earthly branches, i.e. on the animal years under which the couple were born. These animal sign readings may appear superficial but they are remarkably accurate in categorizing the level of compatibility.

ANTIDOTES FOR HOROSCOPE INCOMPATIBILITY

Where a horoscope indicates incompatibility I believe that the correct use of Feng Shui can mitigate such a situation. According to Feng Shui masters, incompatibility between two people based on their birth charts can be appeased. The best ways of doing this are by having marriage harmony symbols in the bridal bedroom, and by the correct exchange of gifts between the bride and groom during the marriage ceremony.

The best of these symbols are the double happiness sign and the pair of geese or mandarin ducks (*see* pages 64 and 63). It is also excellent for the couple to sleep with their heads pointed to the nien yen direction (*see* page 69). Doing this creates harmony. If the nien yen directions of the couple differ, as they definitely will if they are incompatible, choose to use the husband's direction. It is the husband's luck that will reflect on the state of the marriage.

EXCHANGING GIFTS AS AN ANTIDOTE

A correct exchange of gifts based on the practice of symbolic Feng Shui can help to mitigate some of the obstacles represented by incompatible horoscope charts. The source of incompatibility is usually due to a clashing of the five elements. Thus, if the bride's horoscope lacks the element of water and that of the bridegroom's has an excess of earth, then because earth destroys water, the marriage will cause the bride to die of thirst through lack of water.

A gift from the bridegroom to the bride at the time of marriage that suggests the water element symbolizes that the marriage will make things more harmonious between them. A suitable gift would be, for example, a pair of blue shoes, a black evening dress, blue sapphire earrings, blue eye shadow, a set of blue bed sheets, or a pair of goldfish in a small aquarium. Each of these suggestions is positive because it manifests the water element.

The bride can undertake the same analysis when selecting gifts for her husband. Gifts such as those recommended above are not the traditional good fortune gifts given as part of the marriage ritual. They are modern-day adaptations based on the theory and method of *wu xing* or five element compensation.

BEFORE UNDERTAKING A MARRIAGE HOROSCOPE, EACH PERSON NEEDS TO DISCOVER THE ANIMAL YEAR IN WHICH HE OR SHE WAS BORN.

Suggestions for the other four elements are as follows:

- To compensate for a lack of fire, give red outfits, rubies, coral, garnets or cornelians, chandeliers, and lights.
- To compensate for a lack of earth, give all kinds of semiprecious gems and crystal.
- To compensate for a lack of wood, give silk flowers, paintings of auspicious flowers, and healthy leafy plants.
- To help compensate for a lack of metal, give plenty of gold.

Wedding Ceremonies

There are so many "auspicious rituals" related to the marriage ceremony that it is impossible to follow them all. Highlighted here are some of the more important marriage practices that can be incorporated into modern-day weddings, especially those relating to the future happiness of the couple.

THE CEREMONIAL WEDDING DRESS

In Chinese weddings, the bride is usually elaborately made up and dressed in a red *qua*. This is the ceremonial wedding dress and it is usually decorated with beads, crystals, and sometimes even with precious stones. The *qua* would have elaborate embroidery that features the auspicious dragon phoenix or peonies and other symbols of good fortune. Wearing this ceremonial wedding dress is significant and auspicious for the couple and especially for the bride. Only the first wife is entitled to wear it, however, since this signifies her special and new status in the husband's family.

I strongly advise Chinese brides, no matter how modern they may be, to get married in a *qua* since it is most auspicious to do so. These dresses can be exceptionally beautiful. But do not buy a *qua* until you have definite marriage plans. An old wives' tale suggests that to buy a *qua* prematurely or even to buy a marriage bed prematurely causes bad luck that negates the chances of getting married. So do not buy an antique wedding bed for your unmarried daughters.

WEDDINGS ARE IMPORTANT OCCASIONS FOR THE USE OF AUSPICIOUS SYMBOLS.

If you do not want a *qua*, getting married in red (or white) is auspicious. Do not wear black – this is much too Yin for what should be a Yang occasion. It could cause a senior relative (such as a father or an uncle) at the celebration to succumb to serious illness that could prove fatal. The Chinese refer to this as being seriously affected by the Yin energy emanated. Remember, too, that the bride must not change into black for her wedding party nor should guests since this is deemed to be very unkind. They may, however, wear red since this heightens the Yang energy.

At the reception, dress the table with auspicious objects, such as the dragon phoenix pair or the double happiness symbol. The bride and groom should then drink a mixture of wine and honey out of glasses tied together with red thread, exchanging goblets and then drinking again. This seals their commitment to each other. At this point the bride can change out of her ceremonial bridal dress into a more comfortable evening *cheongsam*, which should also be red.

MARRIAGE AND RED CARS

In the old days, the groom's party would come and collect the bride in a red marriage sedan chair that would be elaborately decorated with auspicious symbols such as lanterns and firecrackers. Today, the sedan chair is outdated but red continues to be significant. But in its place it is a good idea to travel to the wedding in a red car. If this proves difficult, I recommend that the car is decorated with auspicious symbols. For example, use red satin ribbons to tie an endless knot that symbolizes eternal love, or use a double happiness decal to decorate each side of the car.

Marriage celebrations in the old days often started with a procession of the bride going to the groom's house. The bridal sedan chair would have the groom's family name emblazoned in red characters, and for luck, a bright red umbrella was borne aloft at the front of the procession by family retainers or relatives. In addition, numerous red satin and paper scrolls were

TO FURTHER ENHANCE THE CHANCE OF HAPPINESS, NEWLYWEDS SHOULD DRINK HONEY AND WINE FROM A PAIR OF GLASSES TIED TOGETHER WITH RED RIBBON.

TRADITIONALLY PARENTS GIVE NEWLYWEDS A RED PACKAGE FILLED WITH MONEY AT THE TEA DRINKING CEREMONY DURING THE WEDDING.

carried as placards containing the double happiness characters in gilt to attract good fortune for the occasion. The bride's brothers walked near her chair, while inside her face was hidden by elaborate ceremonial headgear. Firecrackers were let off when the procession arrived at the groom's home. When the bride descended from the chair, the youngest son of the groom's family greeted her by holding a mirror toward her. But the bride had to look down and an elderly lady and attendants would then lead her to the bridal chamber.

The rituals associated with the procession and arrival of the bride at the groom's home – the letting off of firecrackers and the display of auspicious symbols – represented the loud celebration of a *hei see*, a happy occasion. Observing these rituals was believed to attract good Chi that ensured the safe arrival of the bride to the groom's home, and further ensured that she would be happy as a new daughter of her husband's family. This meant that the bride would live harmoniously with her in-laws. A red umbrella signified that her new family would protect her. Her brothers would also walk alongside her, symbolizing that the bride was leaving her old family amicably. Finally, the gifts she brought with her (gold, jewelry, money, and brocades) symbolized that she brought auspicious good fortune to her husband and his family.

THE TEA CEREMONY

A story deriving from an ancient fairy tale involves Tat Mo, the Indian Brahmin generally credited with bringing Buddhism to China. He is also said to be the originator of the tea plant. Legend has it that one day, while meditating, sleep overcame him and he dozed off. When he awoke he was determined that it would never happen again so he cut off his eyelids. These fell to the earth, took root, immediately sprouted, and became the first tea plant. This is why, the elders say, drinking tea keeps you awake and fully alert.

Of course, there are many varieties of tea – from the cooling green teas and the fragrant jasmine teas to the rich black teas. Among Asian cultures, both the Japanese and the Chinese have raised the drinking of tea to an extremely high art form. Drinking tea is a very elaborate production full of protocol and replete with symbolic meanings. Special utensils and teapots are used. Special varieties of teas are drunk in different ways, and special rituals accompany the drinking of tea.

A most important tea drinking ritual is associated with marriage ceremonials. Newly married couples dressed in their wedding finery kneel in front of their respective parents and each offers a small cup of tea after which the parents bless them and offer them a red packet filled with money. The tea offering signifies respect for the parents and is an expression of filial gratitude.

According to custom, the more refined the variety of tea, the more substantial the offering. Likewise, the bigger the red packet in terms of money gift, the more auspicious the start of married life. In the old days, parents of the bride often presented gold to their departing daughter after the tea ceremony. This was deemed an auspicious offering although in modern times this has been replaced with a red packet of money. Tea must also be offered to every member of the family one generation above the couple as an indication of respect to family elders. So no matter how modern you are, you should not do away with this tea ceremony because it brings good luck.

THE DRAGON DANCE

One of the rituals at marriage celebrations during the old days was the dragon dance, which was held to invoke descendants' luck – the issue of many sons to

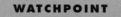

WATCHPOINT

To the Chinese, the tea drinking ceremony symbolizes an eternal wakefulness and alertness.

carry on the family name. Another custom, which seems to have lost its appeal in the light of modern attitudes, used to require the bride upon entering her husband's household for the first time to be carried over a pan of red-hot burning charcoal. This would be laid on the threshold of the door, and the bride would have to be carried by two women whose husbands and children were still alive. This ritual was deemed auspicious because it would ensure the bride would be successful in childbirth, and that there would be no complications that might cause her to die in childbirth.

Up in the bridal chamber, the family matriarch would have arranged for a young virgin boy born in the year of the dragon to roll on the bridal bed three times to activate Yang energy for the couple. Lanterns would have been hung with the double happiness words and the bridal curtain embroidered with the image of many children. These rituals were to ensure a fruitful union resulting in children. Most important would be the presence of the dragon image in the home, preferably images of the Nine Dragons since this reflected the sons of the dragon (*see* page 39).

IMAGES OF THE DRAGON IN THE HOME, SUCH AS IN A WINDOW PANE, SIGNIFY A GREATER CHANCE OF SONS BEING BORN TO THE INHABITANTS.

Celebrating Birthdays

According to many sources of Chinese wisdom, it was deemed unwise to celebrate birthdays with dinner feasts because such a ritual would attract the jealousy of wandering spirits. Thus only a baby's first month was celebrated and thereafter it was discreet to "forget" your birthday – until you reached the grand old age of 60.

AUSPICIOUS GIFTS IN PREGNANCY

According to the *Book of Odes*, an old Chinese classic of customs and folklore, if you are pregnant and you dream of bears – be they black, brown, or white – it indicates you will get a son. If you dream of snakes it is an omen for the birth of a daughter. For many centuries, the Chinese desire for sons was unwavering. Even as recently as this century, parents in China, weighed under by the one child rule, often abandoned baby girls to allow them to try again. Thankfully, this harmful preoccupation is beginning to lose its hold.

There is a very famous painting that shows a hundred children playing in a garden. All the children are boys and this painting is believed to be most auspicious as a gift to a pregnant woman because it sends wishes for many sons. It is said that many masterpieces with this subject used to hang in the bedchambers of the emperors to signal the wish that the son of heaven would produce many male heirs to maintain the dynastic continuation.

The best gifts for a pregnant woman would be auspicious paintings with symbolic meanings. One showing a boy mounted on a unicorn or a boy holding a lotus signified wishes for sons. A painting of 12 children with peaches and pomegranates says may you have a long life and plenty of children. A painting of an old man with a child is considered auspicious since this means wishing the pregnant woman a particularly clever son. The aspiration of giving birth to a clever son capable of performing brilliantly at the Imperial exams has been a prime aspiration of Chinese parents for over 2,000 years. The examinations that were regularly taken were the best way of attaining success and high rank in the emperor's court, a success that would benefit the entire family.

It is not so different in today's world. Education is still the key to great success. So if you want to present a particularly apt gift with this auspicious meaning, give a painting that depicts a dragon, and better yet a dragon carp. This means a carp with the body of a fish but the head of a dragon, which implies the successful crossing of the dragon gate – it is said that the carp swims against the current and leaps over the gate to transform into a dragon. This symbolizes the successful graduation from exams and joining the august ranks of the officials.

FIRST-MONTH CEREMONIALS

In terms of life aspirations, the birth of a son is always regarded as an extremely happy occasion and in China there are specific customs and rituals that take place to

GIFTS OF GOLD BANGLES AND BRACELETS ARE AUSPICIOUS WHEN PRESENTED TO A SMALL BABY.

commemorate the event. This is especially so among the rich and powerful since sons were deemed particularly important to carry on the family name. Girls were regarded as less important since they were expected eventually to marry and leave the family. Thus the birth of sons was always a greater cause for celebration than the birth of daughters. In modern days, of course, we can celebrate both equally intensely and observe all the good fortune rituals equally for both sons and daughters. I know I did when Jennifer was born since she was as precious to me as if I had given birth to a son.

Upon her birth I gave Jennifer a long pink dress. This was because I considered the customary auspicious red to be a bit loud. But I did send eggs dyed red to my parents and my in-laws. Also I celebrated the first-month birthday with a very elaborate dinner when I invited all my friends. This celebration dinner apparently brings good fortune to the family since it announces a *hei see*, which attracts good Chi to the home. It is therefore better to hold the celebration dinner at home since lots of people coming to the home is what attracts Yang energy.

Gifts of gold are given to the baby at this time – bangles, bracelets, and little gold coins are symbolically the most auspicious. When you are invited to a baby's

month-old celebration dinner, therefore, do bring a bit of gold to present to the child. This tradition is far more meaningful than bringing toys or clothes, and probably less expensive too.

FEAST OF A THOUSAND AUTUMNS

The Chinese generally take the attitude that birthdays, unlike marriages and births of sons, are not happy occasions unless it is to celebrate the great birthdays of parents. These are the sixtieth, seventieth, and eightieth birthdays, which are referred to as the feast of a thousand autumns. This implies wishing the birthday patriarch or matriarch to live to a thousand years. Such occasions are indeed causes for celebrating and it is maintained that the bigger these celebrations, the greater the Yang energy generated, and the greater the chances of living to a very old age.

Often during such occasions the children present auspicious longevity symbols as gifts, such as pictures depicting cranes or the Queen of the West (*see* page 53). The most popular is the God of Longevity carved out of a precious material such as jade or some other semiprecious stone or made of porcelain.

BRING A GIFT OF GOLD TO A BABY'S FIRST-MONTH CELEBRATION.

5

GOOD FORTUNE
FLOWERS AND FRUITS

Flowers and fruits are the natural nectar that brings auspicious energies into homes. They signify the growth energies of the wood element and the successful attainment of success. Fruits are the emblem of the final goal while flowers signify the exciting precursor to the harvest. In Feng Shui, there are wealth plants and prosperity fruits. There are also special good fortune flowers. For example, orchids, hyacinths, and narcissus at the New Year signify an illustrious new beginning – the recognition and flowering of hidden talents. Enjoy the practice of Feng Shui by searching for all the good fortune plants that are available in your country.

Good Fortune Flowers

In general, any home that has plenty of healthy flowering plants manifests good Chi energy. Place all the plants with thorns at the edge of your garden and then grow a few varieties of good fortune flowers. It is auspicious to organize the colors of your blooms in accordance with the five elements of your compass direction sectors. Use reds and oranges for the south, white for the west and northwest, blues and violets for the north, and yellows for everywhere else.

In Feng Shui, almost all flowers convey beauty, grace, and perfection but flowers with thorns on their stems are not as popular as those without. For example, as a symbol to express love and affection, the rose does not enjoy the same kind of popularity as the peony. Thus if you wish to send roses to loved ones, make certain the thorns have all been removed. And since we are on the subject of roses, yellow roses are far more auspicious in terms of enhancing a relationship than red roses.

THE FLOWERS OF THE FOUR SEASONS

The flowers of the four seasons represent happiness and good fortune throughout the year. It is an excellent idea to display them in the home to encourage the smooth flow of happy energy.

- At the start of the year, the flowers of spring are the iris and the magnolia.
- In the summer, the peony and the lotus bring good luck.
- In the fall, it is the chrysanthemum that attracts good fortune.
- And in the winter months, it is the plum blossom.

According to the *Book of Odes* (an old Chinese classic that spells out many of the good fortune symbols), doorways benefit from a display of magnolias, and peonies bring great good luck when placed high up. In the fall, orchids should be hung along corridors, and in the winter, blossoms should be placed in large porcelain vases. Chrysanthemums should be

displayed on altars and the lotus should be mixed with lilies in the garden. Most auspicious of all for the young women of the family is a display of peonies. Silk peonies are available in glorious colors and don't fade too quickly. When displayed with plum blossom, for example, in a broad porcelain vase, excellent marriage luck for the daughters of the family is portrayed.

The display of flowers in the home has always been considered as indicating various types of good fortune. Different flowers denote different things, and in the *Book of Odes* there are many descriptions of how flowers are to be displayed. The most important criteria is to remember that flowers should never be allowed to fade while on display in the house. As soon as there are signs of wilting, they should be removed, otherwise they emit harmful Yin energy. In this connection, the use of driftwood in flower arrangements is not regarded as an auspicious arrangement.

MAGNOLIAS

The magnolia is symbolic of feminine beauty and sweetness. It is second in popularity only to the peony

THE MAGNOLIA IS A VERY POPULAR FLOWER BECAUSE IT SYMBOLIZES MARITAL HAPPINESS.

for signifying a beautiful woman and marital happiness. In the old days, only emperors and members of the Imperial family were allowed to cultivate the magnolia plant. Magnolias are superb for wedding bouquets because of their symbolic meaning and because they are white in color. According to the flowers of the four seasons, they are auspicious flowers for spring time.

THE LOTUS

To Buddhists all over the world, the lotus signifies the holy seat of the Lord Buddha. It is one of the eight auspicious objects of Buddhism (*see* pages 112–115). To the Chinese, the lotus symbolizes ultimate purity and perfection because it rises untainted and exquisitely beautiful from the mud. Every part of the lotus plant, from its roots to its flower, can be used, and each part also has deep significance and meanings. At its most esoteric, the lotus plant signifies inward emptiness and outward beauty and this conveys the true nature of reality according to Buddhist philosophy. Thus images of Buddhas are frequently shown seated on a lotus seat.

ACCORDING TO FENG SHUI, FLOWERS ARE THE EMBODIMENT OF GRACE, BEAUTY, AND PERFECTION.

The popular mantra *Om Mani Peh Meh Hone* associated with Kuan Yin, or the Buddha of Compassion, literally means "I pay homage to the jewel in the lotus." In addition, the Hindu God Brahma is always illustrated seated on a lotus flower. The lotus is also a popular Taoist symbol of good fortune. It is the emblem of one of the Eight Immortals who is seen holding a lotus pod, which some say represents descendants' luck (*see* page 51).

AMONG OTHER THINGS, THE LOTUS BLOSSOM SYMBOLIZES ABUNDANCE AND EXAM SUCCESS.

As a symbol of auspicious Chi, the lotus has multiple layers of good meaning stretching from uninterrupted social advancements to examination success and great abundance. What it signifies depends on how it is represented in paintings and good fortune art. Thus, when the lotus is depicted being held by a young man, it indicates success in relationships. A single lotus with one bud signifies perfect union. Shown with a magpie, it offers examination success luck. Illustrated with a boy holding a carp, it means prosperity and abundance.

YELLOW CHRYSANTHEMUMS AND PLUM BLOSSOMS

Yellow chrysanthemums and plum blossoms are wonderful and auspicious flowers either to display, to grow, or to present as a gift to someone. They signify a life of ease, and Buddhists are particularly fond of using these flowers as offerings on altars. During the lunar New Year these are the most auspicious flowers to display. A profusion of yellow chrysanthemums in a long vase or a porcelain urn filled with strong blossom stalks simply conveys so much strong and powerful Yang energy that it instantly attracts good luck into the home. Plum blossoms signify beauty and splendor even in the winter.

TO ATTRACT GOOD LUCK INTO THE HOME, DISPLAY CHRYSANTHEMUMS.

Thus plum blossoms and fruits symbolize beauty in adversity. They also indicate longevity since the flowers are able to bloom on leafless and apparently lifeless branches of the tree even up to an advanced age.

Chrysanthemums signify anything that is long lasting and has durability. Thus love, success, commitments, luck – anything that you wish could last forever – can be augmented by displaying these beautiful fall flowers. When combined with any of the other longevity symbols such as pine or bamboo, or the crane or deer, the indication of longevity is considerably strengthened.

ORCHIDS

Orchids signify perfection and are considered emblematic of the superior man. They also symbolize good family luck and plenty of progeny. In any case, they are emblems of love and beauty, so sending orchids is a safe bet. Violet-colored orchids are said to be most auspicious.

FOR GOOD FAMILY LUCK CHOOSE ORCHIDS.

THE NARCISSUS

The narcissus is an extremely auspicious flowering bulb. Said to bestow the flowering of your hidden talents, this beautiful golden flower is excellent for career people who wish to have their hard work and efforts recognized and rewarded. Grow a bowl of narcissus during the lunar New Year, because this is the time when the plant sends up beautiful flowers. The narcissus is also an excellent gift to wish someone plenty of career luck for the coming year. If you cannot find any narcissus, the hyacinth makes a good substitute.

TO ENSURE YOUR WO EFFORTS ARE RECOGNIZ DISPLAY A NARCISSU

THE LIME PLANT

A lime plant laden with ripe fruit is an image of abundance, especially when placed just outside the main front door. This healthy growing plant brings money luck to any home that grows it, but is considered to be especially auspicious at the lunar New Year. During the 15 days of celebrations, a lime tree placed on each

THE LIME PLANT ATTRACTS MONEY LUCK WHEN DISPLAYED OUTSIDE THE MAIN DOOR.

side of the main door brings prosperity luck throughout the coming year.

The origin of this symbolism lies in the Chinese preoccupation with oranges. During the time of the Ming emperors, annual tributes of oranges were sent to the Imperial capital from the southern provinces. Because of the long journey to the capital, these auspicious fruits were transported in the form of potted plants so that by the time they arrived in Beijing, the fruits had ripened and turned an auspicious orange. In Malaysia and Singapore today, many corporate businesses deliver a pair of potted lime trees to their favored customers and important associates during the New Year as a gesture of appreciation for business given through the year. Local nurseries have also perfected the art of getting the plants to flower at precisely the right time so that during the New Year, the fruits would have ripened.

THE JADE PLANT

I was told years ago that the Chinese value the jade plant highly because it signifies the tree of wealth or money plant. I never gave it much credence until I started writing Feng Shui books and became increasingly observant and aware of my surroundings. That was when I started noticing just how many Chinese restaurants in London had these plants. These plants are placed near the entrance to

THE JADE PLANT IS ALSO KNOWN AS THE MONEY PLANT, SIGNIFYING GREAT GOOD FORTUNE AND WEALTH.

restaurants to create success luck for the business. They are also good when placed in the southeast to energize the money luck of this corner.

I first heard of the jade plant while based in Hong Kong many years ago. It was explained to me that the succulent leaves of the plant resembled jade, a precious stone highly valued by the Chinese for its many attributes. A jade plant was thus the nearest thing to the wish-fulfilling gem tree so highly prized as a decorative object of great excellence (see page 106). In recent years many of these gem trees have come out of South Africa. They are made of gold wire and a variety of semiprecious stones that include jasper, cornelian, natural crystals, and amethysts. These gem trees simulate the jade plant but, of course, for those of you who can find such a plant there is nothing like the real thing.

Good substitutes for the jade plant are other species of succulent cactus plants, whose leaves are thick with water. These even look prosperous. Do not mix them up with the thorny cactus, however, because they are not at all auspicious. Indeed, any plants with sharp pointed thorns are said to send out slivers of poison arrows that create bad luck so thorny plants are best confined to the edges of the garden where they can repel unwanted visitors and protect the house.

In Malaysia and Singapore a variety of plant that is regarded as a money plant is the creeper with heart-shaped leaves that can be grown both indoors or out. These money plants grow very easily in water. Their leaves are green and yellow and they are best grown in the east or southeast. Outdoors, these plants can sometimes magnify in size and become huge creeper plants that cling onto trees as parasitic plants. They lose their auspicious attributes when grown in this way.

Good Fortune Fruits

As there are good fortune flowers, so there are good fortune fruits, which may be displayed lavishly, in fruit bowls or as images in pictures and sculptures. The most significant good fortune fruits are the pomegranate, the orange, the lichee, and the persimmon, each bringing its own special kind of luck.

THE POMEGRANATE

The pomegranate is a popular and lucky fruit. This fruit comes in shades of brilliant reds, and it bursts open to reveal plenty of seeds. This is the reason it is regarded as a symbol of fertility. The fruit is said to create the luck for many sons.

The pomegranate also symbolizes a family that is blessed with good and filial children who will each grow up to bring honor and glory to the family. When a pomegranate is eaten during the New Year, it is said that mothers can expect to give birth to sons during the course of the year. The pomegranate plant is highly prized by Buddhists who use it in their prayer rituals.

IF YOU WANT TO CONCEIVE A CHILD, YOU SHOULD DISPLAY THE POMEGRANATE IN YOUR HOME.

THE ORANGE

The orange is regarded as being a fruit that signifies gold – which, in turn, is another word for extreme good fortune. Since it is gold, the orange is considered to be extremely auspicious and is thus a de rigeur part of the New Year festivities. In fact, New Year is considered incomplete without the orange because the word for orange is *kum*, which is also the word for gold.

There are many varieties of oranges in China: the popular variety used for the New Year celebrations is the brightly colored mandarin orange. Other auspicious varieties are the cinnabar-colored variety, which some say is similar to the peach fruit of immortality (*see* page 56). Such colored oranges are thought to have been used in Taoist alchemy.

It is a good idea to display oranges lavishly in the home during the 15 days of the lunar New Year. This ensures that there will be happiness and prosperity in the household throughout the coming 12 months.

> **WATCHPOINT**
>
> Oranges are given to relatives and friends to wish them prosperity for the coming 12 months.

AT THE LUNAR NEW YEAR DISPLAY ORANGES TO ENCOURAGE MONEY TO FLOW INTO YOUR LIFE.

Those people with altars can place nine oranges stuck with red paper as offerings to their Buddhas and deities. This too is considered auspicious since it signifies offering gold to the deities. Meanwhile, the peel of the orange is regarded as having medicinal qualities. Dried orange peel is a favorite cure for all kinds of stomach ailments and is also used as a sedative.

THE LICHEE

When the lichee is drawn with the longan it is reputed to signify a marriage union that is blessed with clever children. Young married women are encouraged to eat the lichee and longan fruit to create this luck for themselves. The lichee is also regarded as a symbol of shrewdness and is thus considered good for business people. Paintings of auspicious fruits should always include the lichee.

THE PERSIMMON

The persimmon is an extremely fortunate fruit with wonderful meaning for those with a career in business. As a plant, the persimmon has several lucky attributes. It is said to signify longevity, kindness, and astuteness. The persimmon plant is therefore found in many gardens. It also possesses other auspicious meanings, especially when displayed with other symbols of good fortune.

Thus when placed with mandarin oranges, the combined symbolism means success in all business ventures. It is for this reason that Hong Kong restaurants knowledgeable about the symbolism of fruits often serve tangerines with persimmons as a gesture of good wishes for business success to their corporate customers at the end of a meal. In the same way, persimmon served with the lichee fruit signifies profit

THE PERSIMMON SYMBOLIZES GOOD LUCK FOR BUSINESSES. IT IS EVEN MORE AUSPICIOUS WHEN DISPLAYED WITH MAGNOLIAS.

being made from trading. Once again, it is an auspicious business indication.

In paintings, the persimmon fruit is also frequently drawn with other symbols of good fortune. Thus when the persimmon is featured with magnolias and magic mushrooms the meaning is once again success in business. It is therefore recommended to make gifts of persimmons to your business associates, customers, and partners.

6

SYMBOLS OF PROTECTION

Incorporating symbols of protection into the environment of the living and work space is a significant branch of the practice of Chinese Feng Shui. In China, door gods and fu dogs usually symbolically guard the temples and palaces of the Imperial family as well as the homes of high-level officials. Always displayed as a pair, fu dogs are legendary creatures that are often mistaken for unicorns. Some regard them as lions, others as a combination of several auspicious creatures. There are other protective symbols, too, such as the tiger and the eagle. Learn how to use cures and antidotes to Feng Shui problems, thereby protecting against bad luck and misfortunes.

Protective Animals

The use of symbolism is an integral part of Feng Shui practice, and animal symbolism is particularly effective in protecting the family from physical harm and anxiety. The white tiger, the Chinese lion, and the fu dogs are all formidable creatures; as symbols they work best outside, protecting the home and family from ill-fortune and suffering.

THE WHITE TIGER

The great practice of Feng Shui can be described as the auspicious meeting of the dragon and the tiger – the two great forces of the universe that reflect the primordial Yin and Yang of existence. To the Chinese, the tiger is the emblem of dignity, sternness, courage, and ferocity. It is Yin where the dragon is Yang.

The white tiger brings great good fortune when paired with the celestial dragon and it also protects. It signifies the compass direction of the west, and in terms of orientation, the intangible spirit of the tiger is said to be on the right-hand side of the main door when standing at the door and looking outward. Usually, it is not advisable to place the image of the tiger inside the home, for this creature can turn its ferocity against the house. Unless residents are born in animal years of the tiger or dragon, this danger becomes very real. In a tiger year, the tiger presence in the house in the form of paintings or sculptures can be dangerous omens of accidents and illness.

The tiger is best regarded as a symbol of protection and for this it is good to place his image outside the house by the side of the main door. This ensures that people with bad intentions toward the resident family and its members do not gain entry. One of the best

THE WHITE TIGER IS THE EPITOME OF DIGNITY AND COURAGE.

symbols of protection is said to be a picture of three white tigers, and this should be hung outside the house near the vicinity of the front door. In Taoist temples, doors are frequently decorated with the image of the white tiger for their protective qualities.

In certain parts of China and Asia, the tiger is regarded as the God of Wealth, and it is probably not a coincidence that the most popular God of Wealth, known as Tsai Shen Yeh, is frequently depicted sitting on a tiger. Such an image symbolizes the supremacy of the intangible forces of the dragon resulting in the successful harnessing of the tiger's intangible spirit. If you display this image in your home, your family will be strongly protected from poverty and during good times the white tiger brings great prosperity (*see also* pages 11 and 130).

A PAIR OF LIONS

The lion is not indigenous to China and it is speculated that its image came with the rise in influence of Buddhism. This is because the lion is sacred to Buddhism and is often shown offering flowers to Buddha. The lion is regarded as an emblem of courage, boldness, and bravery. It is a valiant creature that possesses prudence and sagacity. The Buddha Manjushuri is sometimes depicted seated astride a lion,

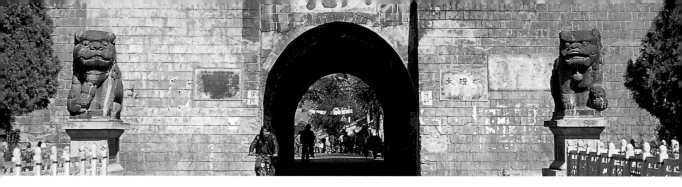

his right hand wielding the sword of wisdom. In the old days, top military officials of the second grade had lion images embroidered onto their court robes.

The lion is also said to be an excellent guardian protector of buildings, particularly sacred buildings – hence the frequency of its usage as temple protector. Large sculpted stone lions are placed flanking main doors, usually one on either side of the door. They are also situated along entrance corridors and guarding the porticos of homes. Sometimes they can be seen guarding the tombs of ancestral graves.

The protective Chinese lion looks formidable. It is drawn with big eyes and a fierce countenance, but it is not generally regarded as a formidable beast. The lion is not as greatly feared as the tiger. Chinese lions also bear little resemblance to African lions. They look more like the other great protectors, the homegrown fu dogs. But it is easy to tell them apart. Chinese lions are almost always sculpted with both front feet on the ground. Sometimes one foot is raised in a menacing way to intimidate demon spirits. For protection against intangible forces, place a pair of lions flanking your main door outside.

IN CHINA, A PAIR OF STONE LIONS ARE FREQUENTLY SEEN FLANKING THE MAIN DOORS OF TEMPLES TO PROTECT THE BUILDINGS.

with evil intentions from entering the house. Fu dogs look remarkably similar to lions but there are subtle differences. For example, fu dogs are mythical creatures frequently shown playing with a ball, which may be the sun, the Yin-Yang egg symbol, or simply a precious stone or a pearl. It is the male fu dog that plays with the ball. Sometimes two fu dogs are shown playing and frolicking and this representation is often compared to two dragons playing with a pearl.

There are many different images and representations of fu dogs in the Forbidden City in Beijing. Fu dogs were deemed excellent protectors for palaces, and homes of the emperors, as opposed to lions, which are more suitable for places of meditation and worship. Fu dogs are more suitable for residential homes.

IN THE FORBIDDEN CITY THERE ARE MANY IMAGES OF FU DOGS.

Choose ceramic fu dogs that differentiate between the male and the female, and always place them with the male (the one with the ball) on the right-hand side of the door (inside looking out) and the female on the other side. It is not necessary to get them too large, but it is a good idea to place them fairly high up. I put mine above the gate and facing each other. All postures are suitable as Feng Shui protector images. The fu dogs can be made of any material although I prefer them to be made of ceramics because these signify earth and Feng Shui is about harnessing good earth energy.

A PAIR OF FU DOGS

Feng Shui masters freely recommend the placement of a pair of fu dogs at the front entrance door since they afford symbolic protection against killing Chi. They are believed to ward off killing energy and prevent people

Symbolic Gods and Heavenly Kings

O nce when I was young, I went with my grandmother to the temple and saw colorful and fierce-looking door gods. My grandmother explained they were meant to keep out bad spirits. Years later in Hong Kong, I found some antique doors with pictures of these deities and, succumbing to nostalgia, I bought them on the spot to guard my home.

DOOR GODS FOR PROTECTION

Military door gods originated in the Tang Dynasty. They are based on two loyal generals, Chin and Yu, who stood guard over the emperor's quarters through the night to ensure the son of heaven would sleep peacefully and not be disturbed by either spirits or ghosts. However, they soon succumbed to their nocturnal duties so the emperor hit on the idea of painting their images onto the entrance doors into his private quarters. Court painters were commissioned to draw two pictures of fully armed generals carrying weapons. The generals eventually came to be known as military door gods and with the passage of time they were drawn one with a white face and one with a black face. The practice became popular and continued to be observed well into the past century.

A less frightening version is that of the civilian door gods, who look less threatening. These gods are also displayed in a pair but they tend to be drawn in court robes giving them the appearance of courtiers rather than fighters. Their protective powers are deemed symbolic rather than actual and they guard against bad luck rather than ghosts and spirits.

A FU DOG WOULD PROTECT THE IMPERIAL FAMILY FROM HOSTILE SPIRITS.

Those who want to revive this old custom of painting door gods on their homes might want to consider these civilian gods rather than the military version. If you do have these gods painted on your front doors, make sure the doors are painted red.

THE GOD OF WAR

Of the many colorful deities of the Chinese pantheon there is probably none as popular or as colorful as the God of War, Kuan Kung, who is also regarded as a God of Wealth. Among his many other titles, he is the protector of the oppressed, guardian deity of the triads, and in recent times, protector of politicians and business leaders alike. Images of Kuan Kung sell like hot cakes. Whether standing or sitting, on horseback, or glaring at his enemies, Kuan Kung in your house brings with it his powerful energy.

The more fierce his countenance, the more powerful he is said to be. Do not lose either his big staff or his sword since these are his weapons, and make sure you place them onto his image correctly. Some of the benefits of having Kuan Kung in the house include peace and harmony for the residents, awesome protection for the patriarch, and prosperity luck for all.

Kuan Kung is most powerful when placed in the northwest corner of a house. He should always face the main door, so that he has his eye on who comes in and out of the home.

THE FOUR HEAVENLY KINGS

The Four Heavenly Kings are known also as Dharma Protectors by Mahayana Buddhists, and as Deva Kings in Sanskrit by the Hindus. These four celestial beings are fabled to be the guardians of the slopes of Mount Meru, a Buddhist paradise. From there, they supposedly protect the universe against attacks by the evil forces and spirits of the four directions.

They are usually depicted as being heavily armed, each holding a personalized weapon that has vast supernatural powers. With them in your home, it is believed that righteousness, honesty, and good moral character will prevail.

Place the Heavenly Kings correctly, either facing the direction or situated in the location that corresponds to their individual domains. Place them on either side of your altar. Or, if you have a holy stupa to house relics of your holy masters, mantras, or other precious objects in your home, place the Heavenly Kings on each corner facing the four cardinal directions.

**THE FOUR HEAVENLY KINGS WARD OFF
NEGATIVE INFLUENCES FROM ALL DIRECTIONS.**

The guardian of the east is Mo Li Ching. He has a white face, a fierce expression, and a beard that looks like copper wire. He carries a spear and a magic sword that has the characters earth, water, fire, and wind on its blade. His weapon symbolizes metal, which overcomes the wood element of the east. Thus does he exercise control over the east. His sword is described as having the power to create a black wind, which produces a million spears that pierce through the bodies of evil nagas, turning them into dust. The wind is followed by fire, which fills the space with a million serpents. He is the most senior of the four kings. Place him in the east of the space you wish to protect.

The guardian of the west is Mo Li Hai. He has a blue face and carries a four-string guitar that, when strummed, causes great balls of fire to drop onto those who would dare to invade the space. In the cycle of elements, fire destroys metal (the element of the west) and it is in this way that he controls his domain. Place him in the west of your home or in the west corner of the altar.

The guardian of the south is Mo Li Hung. He has a red face and he holds the magic umbrella. When opened, the umbrella creates total darkness, and when reversed, it creates huge earthquakes and tidal waves that completely destroy all negative and killing forces.

The guardian of the north is Mo Li Shou. He has a black face and carries a pearl in one hand and a snake in the other. Sometimes this king is shown with an elephant or a white rat. He should be placed in the north to overcome all bad influences from that direction.

Amulets and Charms

The Chinese have used charms and amulets to ward off danger, ill-luck, and bad people throughout the country's recorded history to the present day. Wearing good fortune symbols and symbols of protection effectively complements Feng Shui practice, both in activating good luck and warding off bad Chi.

TAOIST AMULETS FOR PHYSICAL SAFETY

In addition to bringing good luck, Feng Shui offers protection against bad luck, which can come in different guises. An interesting branch of Feng Shui involves harnessing all the methods used in the past to ward off negative Chi that brings accidents, illness, robbery, and physical discomforts. In the old days, the use of Taoist amulets was both widespread and popular. Thus different types of talismans are referred to in the oldest Chinese texts.

Various materials were used in the fashioning of these talismans, and rice paper colored yellow or green was the most popular. Special characters deemed to have the power to keep bad luck at bay were then written on these pieces of rice paper. Such talismans were credited with the power of dissolving bad Chi that was caused by wandering bad spirits.

Different characters could also be written for different purposes. There were special protec-

CHINESE COIN AMULETS ARE EXCELLENT FOR ACTIVATING WEALTH LUCK.

tion amulets for pregnant women; for protection against accidents, against fire, against water, and so forth. Handwritten amulets were believed to be especially powerful for warding off physical harm, giving protection from being assaulted and even against armed robberies.

DRAGON AMULETS CAN CLEANSE HOMES AFFLICTED WITH NEGATIVE CHI.

My Feng Shui master, Mr. Yap Cheng Hai, is particularly adept at writing these protective amulets. He draws his special characters on green paper after chanting some Taoist prayers. I have carried Mr. Yap's protective amulets for over 20 years and have found that they are extremely potent for warding off all kinds of physical harm. I have also frequently asked him to give amulets such as these to friends of mine – which he gladly does and for no charge at all, such is his generosity.

Mr. Yap does things like this on a totally non-commercial basis. Those of you who are fortunate enough to know or meet him can ask him for such an amulet and if he happens to have a spare one about his person he is certain to give it to you. He is really that kind and generous.

DRAGONS AND COINS AS TALISMANS

The use of protective talismans is part of the cultural backdrop against which Feng Shui practice can be studied and understood. On the one hand, wearing talismans can be regarded as superstition. On the other, because they are so much a part of the traditional protective mentality of the Chinese, they seem to complement neatly the practice of Feng Shui, and indeed are even regarded as an adjunct of symbolic Feng Shui. Another important observation I have made throughout my years of investigation into Feng Shui is the fact that almost all the authentic practicing masters of Feng Shui have at least some knowledge of amulets and talismans. This only confirms how closely knit these two areas have become.

All are familiar with using some form of protection. Indeed, many have explained to me that Feng Shui consultants often encountered hazards in the course of their work, so that carrying symbolic protection was something all Feng Shui practitioners knew about. Sometimes it is possible that negative spirits and influences haunt homes where they go to practice Feng Shui, and amulets are believed to protect them from succumbing to illness or other more severe afflictions caused by the dirty energy of such homes. It is for this reason also that Mr. Yap is armed with many types of very powerful talismans given to him by his teachers.

Dragon amulets can be extremely powerful for protecting against being harmed by what is termed dirty energy left over in houses that have had a history of afflicted or bad Feng Shui.

ENHANCE THE POWER OF
CHINESE COIN AMULETS
BY TYING THEM WITH
A LUCKY RED RIBBON.

Symbolic Grids for Protection

I n attempting to unlock the secrets of the eight trigrams that are placed around the Pa Kua, ancient and latter-day Feng Shui scholars focused on the mysterious Lo Shu and Hou Tu grids. In symbolic Feng Shui practice these grids have been imbued with protective potency, especially when displayed with protective animal symbols.

THE LO SHU GRID

The Lo Shu grid (see below) is better known than the Hou Tu grid, and has come to be called the magic square. Its numbers are arranged in such a way that adding them in any direction (horizontally, vertically, or diagonally) results in the number 15. This coincides with one cycle of the waxing and waning moon.

The Lo Shu is regarded as a magic square. Displaying it in conjunction with the noble dragon tortoise is said to attract good Feng Shui. But together they also have the capability of warding off bad forces that are created for individual residents due to harmful orientations based on dates of birth and gender. Over the centuries, this particular compass formula has proved to be very potent when applied correctly. A companion book in this series – *Formulas for Success* (see page 142) – covers the Lo Shu Formula in great detail.

If you live in a house where the orientations of the main door and rooms are not auspicious for you, and you have no choice, try displaying a dragon tortoise with a Lo Shu square stuck at the bottom. Place the dragon tortoise on top of a cupboard, preferably hidden from view, and it should offer protection from such unfortunate orientations.

IT IS BELIEVED THAT THE LO SHU
FORMULA FIRST BECAME APPARENT
ON A TORTOISE SHELL.

THE HOU TU GRID AND DRAGON HORSE

Like the Lo Shu square, the Hou Tu grid of numbers is said to have protective capabilities that can overcome the effect of bad Flying Stars (see illustration, right). Flying Star Feng Shui is a divinitive school of Feng Shui, which is the technique of casting the natal charts of houses based on when they were built or last renovated. This Feng Shui formula tracks the time dimension Feng Shui of homes in that it can predict when bad or good things can happen, depending on where the main door and bedrooms are located. It is based on the premise that every sector of the house has periods of good or bad Feng Shui and these periods can be defined as days, weeks, months, years, or periods of 20 years. The stars are good and bad numbers that move (or fly) from one compass sector of the house to another, thereby bringing with them good luck and bad luck at different times.

Mastering Flying Star Feng Shui is time consuming since it is one of the more complex of Feng Shui formulas, so here is a more straightforward recommendation: overcome the Feng Shui of bad stars by displaying the Hou Tu grid and a dragon horse. I

TO IMPROVE AN INAUSPICIOUS FLYING STAR, DISPLAY A DRAGON HORSE WITH THE HOU TU GRID (BELOW) IN YOUR LIVING ROOM.

One of the things that every Feng Shui practitioner must be wary of is the place of the Five Yellow each year. This is part of Flying Star Feng Shui and it is a major warning taken very seriously. It is located in a different sector each year and suitable precautions are usually recommended to make sure you are not hurt by it. In the year 2000, for example, the Five Yellow is located in the north and thus all through the year you should not energize this spot with new water. If you already have water in the north, leave it there but do not do any digging and cutting in the sector during the year 2000.

Expert practitioners of Flying Stars such as Master Yap Cheng Hai say that one way of overcoming the influence and effect of the Five Yellow (no matter what it is and where it flies to) is to display a large painting of Zhong Kui. The most famous of Chinese heroes (he is also considered a deity by some), Zhong Kui is thought to overcome black magic spells. He is also considered an exorcist of the highest ability since he is said to have 84,000 demon spirits under his command. The best time to invite him into the home is to hang up his picture on the fifth day of the fifth month according to the Chinese calendar. He is best placed near the front door so he can see everyone coming into the home. Or if you wish, you can be like me and place him on the wall at the foot of the stairs. In this way he protects all our upstairs bedrooms from being affected by the Five Yellow.

Zhong Kui is frequently depicted as being exceptionally ugly and with a black face. He is sometimes shown surrounded by urns of wine for he is said to be almost always drunk. The story of his life and how he came to be what he became is a popular Chinese folk tale.

recommend using the Hou Tu grid rather than the Lo Shu because, although Flying Star Feng Shui is generally based on the Lo Shu square, more advanced interpretations use the Hou Tu chart to determine good and bad dates. The Hou Tu is believed to be the key that determines the good and bad dates for individuals.

Copy the Hou Tu numbers arranged as below and place the grid next to the dragon horse – then display both in the living room diagonally opposite the main door with the horse seeming to be looking at the door.

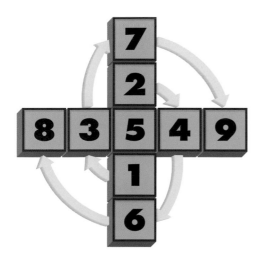

Mirrors, Fans, and Singing Bowls

I have always carried a special and symbolically protective fan and mirror in my handbag. The mirror is an excellent way to deflect bad energy away from me, while my fan shields me from bad Chi. There are many superstitions associated with mirrors and fans, and it is important to learn how they are best used as symbols of good fortune and protection.

THE PA KUA MIRROR

The Pa Kua mirror is probably the best known of all the Feng Shui symbols of protection, but it is also one that has been the most incorrectly used. This eight-sided shape drawn with the eight trigrams allocated around the eight sides according to the Earlier Heaven Arrangement has a mirror in the center.

This mirror is believed to reflect back whatever bad vibes or energy come against your house. Thus if a sharp, pointed, or hostile structure directly faces your main door, then placing the Pa Kua mirror directly above your door outside and facing the structure will send all bad energy back to where it came from, thereby protecting the door and the house.

But the mirror must be hung outside the home and it must never face in. It should also never be hung anywhere inside the home since it also sends out powerful killing energy of its own that will hurt residents who confront or face it directly.

The mirror that is placed in the center of the Pa Kua can be convex, concave, or flat. Pa Kuas with convex mirrors protrude outward and these mirrors reflect and send back the negative energy. It is the most harmful of the three types of mirrors and the one I recommend the least of all.

Pa Kuas with concave mirrors are depressed inward and they absorb and draw all the bad energy into themselves. This is the least harmful of the three types of mirrors and the one I recommend the most since it corrects the bad Feng Shui without sending out too much negative energy of its own. Pa Kuas with flat mirrors are the most common and these neither absorb nor double any bad energy being reflected back.

WATCHPOINT

If you give a mirror to a career person, he or she will enjoy a leap into high office.

SMALL HANDMIRRORS

An old tale from my great-grandmother's day explains that mirrors make spirits visible. For many years my mother carried a mirror given to her by my great-grandmother – a mirror she insists protects her from being charmed and from being cheated by "bad" people. It is a very small handmirror made of silver with very pretty engravings.

She gave it to me when I graduated from university and I used it as a makeup mirror for many years. Then last year, when I went on a pilgrimage of sorts to the Solu Khumbu region of the Himalayas, I parted with my mirror. I was visiting the stupa that contained the relics of the holy lama of that region – a lama who has reincarnated and is now my holy lama in this life. Something made me place the mirror there at the stupa as a kind of offering because I did not have anything else that was suitable on me. It was a totally spontaneous action since I knew that giving mirrors to someone means good luck. So I believed it made a suitable and respectful offering. But I have felt the lack of my personal mirror ever since that auspicious day and have been trying to find something similar to use in its place.

There are many superstitious beliefs associated with mirrors. It is said that if you look into your mirror and cannot recognize yourself, it means you will soon succumb to an illness. It is bad luck to have mirrors in the bedroom directly reflecting the bed. It is also bad luck to dream of mirrors in the night but very fortunate when you dream of a mirror reflecting the sun or sunlight. If you receive one as a gift it means you will soon get married, have a son, or get a promotion. In any case, it means good luck. If you give a mirror as a gift to a career person it means he or she will soon enjoy a quantum and unexpected leap into high office.

Decorative mirrors made of bronze, silver, or gold have been used in China and carried by the women of high families ever since the second millennium B.C.E. There are many stories of how these mirrors were actually magic mirrors capable of protecting the women from harm. Mirrors also feature strongly in Buddhist rituals used by high lamas and monks in their purification ceremonies and prayer sessions. The best magic mirrors were said to be those that were made on auspicious days from special sand taken from central China.

A SANDALWOOD FAN

When I first started lecturing on Feng Shui around the world I used to carry a sandalwood fan with me since this is supposed to ward off bad energy that is inadvertently sent your way. Mr. Yap Cheng Hai told me to carry a fan since this would simulate a screening effect that would deflect any negative energy. He explained that fans were supposed to have the power to deflect hostile Chi. The Chinese regard the fan as wind in paper since it is mostly made of paper stuck on sandal wood. But fans also come in tortoiseshell since this is supposed to enhance its esoteric powers of protection.

Fans have been used since ancient times. There are many variations and they come in a variety of shapes, although round is popular. The folding variety is a Japanese invention introduced into China in the eleventh century through Korea. Irrespective of their shapes, the fan is a popular accessory carried by both men and women. Men carried fans in their sleeves or waistband. They often brought out their fans while discussing matters of court, as much to empha-size their viewpoint as to create an invisible shield that would serve to protect them against people with dishonorable or bad intentions toward them. In the atmosphere of court intrigues, fans were considered an important and significant tool. Taoist masters often painted amulets onto specially created and personal-ized fans for dignitaries of the court.

Scented – especially sandalwood – fans are a great favorite with women because of the special attributes of the perfumed wood. Very intricately cut-out designs on sandalwood fans can be found in Chinese arts and crafts stores in Hong Kong and China. They are usually fashioned into folding fans that can be conveniently carried in a lady's handbag.

INCENSE BLOCKS AND SINGING BOWLS

One of the best methods of ensuring continuously good Feng Shui for your home is to undertake regular space cleansing and purification rituals. The best and easiest way of doing this is to use incense or aroma sticks but I use powdered sandalwood incense blocks. The Malay name is *kemenyem* and they can be bought from almost any shop selling incense sticks and praying accessories.

The incense blocks that I use are made of sandalwood and fash-ioned to resemble gold ingots and I burn them on a special incense

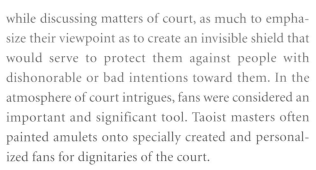

RUN THE WOODEN MALLET
AROUND THE RIM OF THE
SINGING BOWL IN A
CLOCKWISE DIRECTION
TO MAKE IT SING.

BURNING INCENSE STICKS IS THE
EASIEST WAY OF CLEANSING AND
PURIFYING YOUR HOME.

container. Sometimes I also sprinkle special Himalayan mountaintop incense to obtain the pure energy of the Himalayas, but these are very hard to get and also very expensive. I walk around each room of my home in a clockwise direction; and as I do this I let the incense clean and purify dark corners where bad Chi might have inadvertently been accumulating. I allow the smoke from the incense to purify the space. I do this once a month and also whenever there has been a particularly loud quarrel between residents. This cleans all the anger energy and restores harmony once again. I also chant my favorite mantras as I move from room to room with my incense.

I have been told by my friend Denise Linn (a famous and wonderful practitioner of space cleansing as taught by Native Americans) that this is similar to the Native American practice of cleansing homes with smoke made from burning pine branches. Of course, pine branches always give off a marvelous herbal scent, which must be so wonderful for making the energies crisp and clean once more.

THE SINGING BOWL

Another excellent item that I have discovered for space clearing is the singing bowl. This beautiful object creates the most sensational sound vibrations that systematically cleanse the energies of the living space. You can actually feel the energy of the home becoming lighter and happier. For the singing bowl to work, however, it has to be made from seven types of metals, which must include gold and silver (just a tiny bit otherwise they would be very expensive). The actual mix of the metals is a closely guarded secret but I am lucky in that I have found an old-time manufacturer from Katmandu to make these bowls for me.

I highly recommend getting hold of a singing bowl since they can be used to create sensationally crisp energy in your home. I have a hundred of them as well as a huge crystal singing bowl. When I first started using singing bowls to purify my space, the sounds came out rough and flat but over time, as I used the bowls more and more, the sounds have become purer and purer. This has also coincided with the feeling of harmony among family members getting stronger as well.

To bring out the sounds of the singing bowl use a wooden mallet that is made of soft wood. It is also a good idea to let the bowl sit on a small cloth cushion since this improves the sound considerably.

There are two ways to get the bowl to sing. The first way is to strike the bowl firmly with the mallet. Practice several times until you get a sound that is long and sustaining, then walk around the rooms in a clockwise direction and as you strike the bowl feel the sound vibrations getting purer and purer.

The second way is a little difficult to start with but it gets a more refined version of the singing sound. Use the wooden mallet and press it against the outside rim of the bowl then firmly (but without exerting too much pressure) rub the bowl in a clockwise direction. At first you will hear nothing but as you learn how to vary your pressure the bowl will soon start to sing.

If you find it hard to find a singing bowl, you can use a metal bell as a substitute. Use a wooden mallet in the same way to make the bell sing and use the sound to purify the energies of your home. Remember that the secret is to use pressure, but you should never use too much pressure.

7

FENG SHUI PROSPERITY ENHANCERS

Four symbols that are said to attract great good fortune into any home include the wish-granting tree, the wish-fulfilling cow, the precious mountain, and the unharvested harvest. Wind chimes, water features, and lights also play a major role in enhancing Feng Shui prosperity. Old paintings of these subjects are highly valued, especially when they have been hanging in the home of a rich family.

Prosperity Enhancers

The wish-granting tree gave rise to the gem tree, which has enjoyed a huge revival of popularity since South Africa started exporting beautiful "gem trees" made of semiprecious stones. The wish-fulfilling cow has always been a great favorite with Chinese landowners. The unharvested harvest depicts a huge fortune waiting to be plucked. This symbolizes the ripening of prosperity, as if your time to be rich has come. The precious mountain is believed to be a repository of great wealth. Other popular Feng Shui enhancers include wind chimes, which energize the west and the northwest; wealth-bringing water features, which enhance the luck of the east, the southeast, and the north; and bright Yang energy lights and chandeliers that magnify the luck of the south.

PLANT A WISH-GRANTING TREE

Trees play an extremely important role in the practice of Feng Shui. As a deflector of bad energy they can be quite excellent tools for overcoming the onslaught of killing Chi. Thus if your front door is being "hit" by poison arrows from across the road, plant a bushy tree to block the arrow completely from view. These arrows can be straight roads, the triangular rooflines of houses across the street, or they can be anything sharp, straight, or hostile. Sometimes, even the edges of large buildings can create the bad energy of poison arrows. All these hostile structures that bring ill-fortune and bad luck can be completely deflected by planting a tree in a strategic spot that enables the source of the arrow to be blocked off from view.

But the tree is even more effective when it is planted at a spot in the yard that transforms it into the wish-granting tree. According to Feng Shui texts, the potency of the tree in bringing auspicious good fortune depends on three things:

- the spot where it is planted,
- what type of tree it is, and
- what is done to energize the wealth prospects of the tree.

It is best to plant the tree in the east, and to find the right area, take the directions from the center of the house and then measure the 45 degrees that represent the east from the center. The tree – preferably a bushy one with rounded leaves – should be planted in this quadrant. Finally, tie together a thousand coins with red thread and let them hang from the tree.

TREES DEFLECT BAD ENERGY AND CAN ALSO BE TURNED INTO WISH-GRANTING TREES TO INTRODUCE GOOD FORTUNE.

USING THE WISH-FULFILLING COW

I am very fond of telling people the story of my wish-fulfilling cow. It was a crystal ornament presented to me by my staff at the Dao Heng Bank in Hong Kong where I was managing director in the early 1980s. But it was not a cow – it was a bull and it had beautiful specks of 24-carat gold sprinkled inside it. I placed it in a place of honor in the living room of my home, and it brought me a great deal of wealth luck.

The cow is considered an extremely holy animal in places like India and Nepal. But few people realize its true significance. According to Buddhist teachings the cow has the power to transform your wishes into reality provided you treat it with kindness; and provided also that you refrain from eating beef. It is for this reason that so many Buddhist Chinese refrain from eating cow meat or beef. In India, if you bump into a cow and kill it, you can be charged with manslaughter; and in Katmandu cows roam the streets freely because they know they will not get knocked down. Killing a cow with your motor vehicle there can cause you to be imprisoned for murder because the cow is considered to be such a sacred animal. The cow is said to be a holy animal because it provides so much sustenance for the human race.

In Feng Shui, the wish-fulfilling cow is so potent that practitioners place in their houses the image of a cow relaxing on a bed of coins (*see* right). But if you do not have this symbol then look for a painting that includes the cow and hang it in the southeast to energize for the wealth luck that is associated with this corner.

FOR THE MOST AUSPICIOUS FENG SHUI ENERGY, A HOUSE SHOULD BE SITUATED WITH MOUNTAINS OR HILLS BEHIND IT.

DISPLAY THE PRECIOUS MOUNTAIN BEHIND YOU

The mountain is said to be the single most important symbol in Feng Shui because it is a manifestation of all four of the celestial creatures of the four directions. These celestial creatures are the dragon of the east; the phoenix of the south; the tortoise of the north; and the tiger of the west.

Mountains are also said to have a Yin and a Yang aspect and are categorized according to shapes that correspond to the five elements. In general, the mountain is said to represent a wealth of hidden treasure. This is indicated by the trigram ken in the *I Ching*, which describes the mountain as being still, waiting, and prepared.

The mountain contains within it masses of gold and precious things. Thus the mountain is a repository of great wealth. When you can see clear mountain peaks in the distance they are usually indications of various types of good fortune. Thus seeing three mountain peaks in the distance indicates that the eldest son of the family will one day rule the land – indeed, this really is a most powerful omen, especially when it is read with other divinitive signs.

TO ENERGIZE FOR WEALTH LUCK, THE WISH-FULFILLING COW IS BEST POSITIONED IN THE SOUTHEAST.

The best way to use the mountain symbol in Feng Shui is to hang a painting or picture of a mountain behind you at work. This will ensure that in bad economic times you will survive. You will not get laid off nor will you lose out in a political fight within the company. And you will always survive in any strategic one-upmanship in the office. If you are a businessperson you will survive and will not collapse because of bad times. The mountain offers support and protection. Should you want to display the mountain, please make sure there is no water feature in the picture. Any small waterfall in landscape paintings represents water and these would be unsuitable if placed behind you.

FOR THE LUCK OF MATERIAL WELL-BEING TO COME YOUR WAY, DISPLAY A BOWL OF FRESH FRUIT IN YOUR DINING ROOM.

SIMULATE THE ABOUT-TO-BE-HARVESTED FIELD

When you enter any up-market Chinese arts and crafts shop you will find images of freshly harvested fruits made of expensive jadeite, ivory, or ceramics. This is because these fresh and yummy fruits represent the about-to-be-harvested produce of the land.

These are extremely auspicious images, and for obvious reasons: they represent the fruit of the land and displaying them anywhere in your home, and especially in your dining room area, brings the luck of prosperity for the family. The symbolism is that the family will always have more than enough to eat. For the same reason I always recommend hanging beautiful paintings of fresh fruit in the dining room. In Feng Shui, food signifies prosperity.

The display of fruits, freshly plucked from the tree, has its origins in the belief that images of an unplowed harvest are considered to be the luckiest of all food symbols. Thus paintings of fully matured corn fields, rice fields, and wheat fields are excellent for hanging in both the home and office.

In fact, if you are trying to decide on subject matter, look for still life paintings of freshly harvested fruits or fields of ripe corn and wheat. A field of corn or any other cereal food ripe for the plucking symbolizes the crystallizing of hard work.

The time for harvesting is always summer. For this reason, the season of summer represents a flowering and a blooming of efforts. The meanings are most auspicious. Summer is also considered a time of plenty, a time when there is a maximum amount of the precious Yang energy. When you compound this with an image of an unharvested harvest about to bear fruit and food, there cannot be any symbolism more powerful.

HANG WIND CHIMES TO ACTIVATE LUCK

There are two main misconceptions about the hanging of wind chimes in the home. First, some people have heard that wind chimes attract malevolent spirits into the house. However, I have hung wind chimes in my home for 20 years with no problems. Second, it is important to differentiate between using wind chimes to press down on bad luck in certain sectors and using wind chimes to energize for good luck. Some masters advise that solid rods do a better job of pressing down on bad luck; others maintain that the hollow rods are just as efficient, if not more so. More important than solid or hollow rods is the

WIND CHIMES ARE INVALUABLE FOR PRESSING DOWN ON BAD LUCK AND ENERGIZING SECTORS FOR GOOD LUCK.

addition of a pagoda-like structure above them. This feature is said to be most effective in frightening off any bad spirits that may be lurking around because the pagoda is a powerful symbol of protection against bad spirits that may be lurking around. When you use wind chimes to overcome bad luck try to use wind chimes that have five rods.

To energize for good luck, wind chimes work extremely well in the metal element sectors of the house (the west and northwest). This, of course, assumes the use of wind chimes that are made predominantly of metal, e.g. copper, brass, silver, steel, and types of alloys. Wind chimes are particularly powerful when hung to activate the luck of the patriarch in the northwest corner of a living room and office, and for the luck of health and longevity in the west. For energizing purposes remember to use only those with hollow rods.

WATER FEATURES

To benefit from the creation of a water feature in the house please note the following:

• Water features include small ponds, miniature fountains, waterfalls, and aquariums.

• There are only three places that can benefit from the placement of a water feature: the east, the southeast, and the north. Of the three, the most beneficial is the north corner because this sector is representative of the water element. In the east and southeast sectors water benefits the wood element.

• It is advisable not to have water directly behind the house since this generally indicates missed opportunities. However, if your north is behind you, then you can

BEAUTIFUL LIGHTING IN THE GARDEN WILL ATTRACT EXTRA YANG ENERGY TO ENHANCE ROMANCE LUCK.

place a water feature here, but try to orientate it such that it is on either side of the house rather than directly behind the house.

• Make certain that the water feature is not on the right-hand side of the main front door (from inside looking out). Water features should always be to the left of the main door.

YANG ENERGY LIGHTS

One of the most potent of all symbolic enhancers of good fortune energy are bright lights, which bring a huge dose of precious Yang energy. They are a most powerful antidote against many Feng Shui ills. Lights can overcome misplaced toilets and they can dissolve the Shar Chi created by narrow corridors and tight corners. Lights can also be a powerful counter agent for missing corners. But it is as Feng Shui prosperity enhancers that lights are most useful. Thus they can be placed all around a store or business to attract customers and help to double the turnover of the business. Lights are also excellent when used to energize the south sector of the home or living room, especially if red in color. Energizing the south will bring recognition and attract promotion.

The best kind of lighting to use is a crystal chandelier. These light fittings combine two complementary elements – fire and earth – and in the process produce masses of Yang energy that in turn introduce masses of Sheng Chi to a home.

Lights are especially good for romance and marriage luck in the southwest, which is the place of the matriarch. It is best to have such a light in the garden, and you should try to keep it switched on for at least three hours each night.

8

THE EIGHT
AUSPICIOUS OBJECTS

The eight auspicious objects belong to the Buddhist pantheon and are symbols of good fortune. They originated in India and Tibet but they have been enthusiastically embraced by superstitious Chinese who have incorporated them into their practice of Feng Shui.

Auspicious Objects

The first of the eight auspicious objects is the mystic knot, which signifies the state of samsara – a continuous rebirth of humankind. The knot also protects any wealth and success that have already been attained. Then there is the conch, which signifies good travel luck; the double fish, which signifies material wealth; the canopy – a powerful symbol of protection; the lotus, which signifies purity; and the vase, which contains the nectar of bliss and happiness. Finally, the wheel represents the luck of real wisdom and scholarship, and the jar symbolizes the accumulation of family wealth.

THE MYSTIC KNOT

The mystic knot is sometimes also referred to as the endless knot that is said to "swallow its own tail." The more esoteric meaning of this symbol implies there is no beginning and no end – reflecting the Buddhist philosophy that existence is one endless round of birth and rebirth, a state the Buddhists refer to as samsara. The knot is thus a wonderful reminder that once we realize this great noble truth about existence we will start to seek methods to free us of the endless cycle of births and rebirths. This is what is called freedom, the freedom from samsara and freedom from the cycle of rebirths. Buddhists of all traditions seek to attain this freedom. This sign is seen on the breast of the Hindu deity Vishnu, and it is also one of the eight signs on the sole of Buddha's feet.

At a less spiritual level, the mystic knot can be seen as a symbol of a single lifetime because it signifies a long life uninterrupted by illnesses, setbacks, or suffer-ings. From this viewpoint it is also known as the lucky knot. In view of this, it is a very popular ornamental symbol that is used in a variety of ways, carved on furniture, woven into carpets, embroidered on garments, and painted on screens and porcelain.

Its significance in Feng Shui is as an easy-to-use motif that can be incorporated into the design and pattern of grilles, doors, and furniture. It is an excellent symbol of longevity and good health. Some also see it as a perfect emblem for undying love, thus it has also been identified as a lucky love symbol suitable for ensuring that the romance in a marriage will last. It is therefore an excellent motif that can be carved on beds and furniture.

THE CONCH OR COWRIE SHELL

The conch or cowrie shell is a symbol of a prosperous voyage. It signifies great travel luck and is particularly suitable for those who undertake a lot of business travel. The shell is also an insignia of royalty or of royal patronage. Those engaged in the service of serving royalty would benefit from having the shell symbol worked into their house decor.

The shell is also one of the eight auspicious objects since it represents the voice of Buddha. On a spiritual level, the conch signifies the far-reaching essence and depth of the Buddha's teachings. It is also one of the marks on the Buddha's footprints. Buddhists thus consider the shell a lucky object. It is usually mounted

FOR GOOD TRAVEL LUCK – ESPECIALLY
FOR PEOPLE WHO GO AWAY A LOT
FOR BUSINESS – DISPLAY CONCH OR
COWRIE SHELLS IN YOUR HOME.

THE DOUBLE FISH

I have already described the wonderful symbolism of the fish – that it represents abundance, wealth, harmony, and connubial bliss (*see* pages 34–37). When shown as a pair, the fish symbol does not merely signify happiness doubled. It also denotes the joys of physical union between lovers and spouses.

From the Buddhist perspective, the double fish symbol may be viewed as something of an amulet, which when worn either as a pendant or as an article kept in the wallet is a powerful charm capable of averting evil and accidents and preventing you from succumbing to epidemics and bad intentions.

AMONG OTHER THINGS, THE DOUBLE FISH SYMBOL IS USED TO REPRESENT HARMONY AND CONNUBIAL BLISS.

THE CANOPY

The canopy has the significance and meaning of the flag, the banner, and the umbrella; as a result of which it is sometimes drawn as one of these three items. The canopy symbolizes victory in a Buddhist sense where the real enemy is said to be the selfish ego. As a result, the canopy is one of the auspicious signs because Buddhists believe that the successful conquest of a person's ego represents one of the most important

on a rosewood stand, often gilded with gold or silver. From a Feng Shui perspective, the shell can be used to attract business luck from overseas. Those engaged in export trade or whose companies depend on foreign turnover to prosper can consider displaying beautiful cowrie shells. They are inexpensive and suitable as Feng Shui energizers.

The shell is also an excellent symbol for those engaged in work, business, or enterprises that benefit from their being well known and respected. To create the luck of fame and reputation place a fairly large marine specimen (about 6–8in/15–20cm) in the south corner or sector of the living room. The cowrie shell can also be placed in the northeast and southwest to strengthen the energy of these corners. Strong energy in the northeast creates excellent education luck, while strong energy in the southwest enhances and improves relationship luck.

preliminary steps on the path toward gaining the peerless state of enlightenment.

On a more mundane level, the canopy takes on the significance of the Imperial umbrella. It is a token of someone held in the highest respect. It is a symbol of dignity and high rank. In a way the canopy or umbrella represents victory and success in career.

The umbrella is also a symbol of protection from negative influences. The belief is that the placement of an umbrella just outside the front door protects the house from burglars and from strangers with ill intentions. It is also said that umbrellas afford good protection when made of silk, decorated with tassels painted with auspicious signs, and placed inside the house. Such umbrellas should be placed diagonally opposite the front door.

THE LOTUS

The lotus is a symbol of purity and perfection. In Buddhism, the lotus also signifies the attainment of enlightenment. Its petals are said to symbolize the doctrine of Buddha's teachings. Buddha himself is usually depicted seated on a sacred lotus. His posture with a straight back and with the lower limbs folded in front is called the lotus posture. Buddhist monks and holy masters all assume this posture when they meditate and teach the sutras.

The mantra of the Compassionate Buddha – *Om Mani Peh Meh Hone* – is the lotus mantra and reciting it many thousands of times brings a rain of blessings. The Chinese manifestation of the Compassionate Buddha is the Goddess of Mercy, Kuan Yin, and this mantra is thus the Kuan Yin mantra. The Buddha who brought Buddhism to Tibet is called the Lotus Buddha because he is said to have been born from a lotus.

THE WHEEL

The sacred wheel is one of the auspicious signs believed to be on the footprints of Buddha. It is variously

BRINGING THE EIGHT AUSPICIOUS OBJECTS TOGETHER FOR GOOD FORTUNE

Displaying all eight objects together is believed to bring complete good fortune to the household, the kind of good fortune that addresses not only the material luck of the family but also the spiritual luck that brings peace of mind and real happiness. In fact, many Buddhist households display banners and wall hangings that have these eight objects printed or sewn on them for good luck.

The eight symbols can also be displayed collectively as paintings on walls, or better yet they can be drawn as eight separate objects and then embroidered onto heavy materials to be used in front of rooms as door coverings, room dividers, and screens. Thus if your door is too close to the staircase, for example, use a door hanging with the eight objects to overcome the bad Chi. Or if doors are placed one after another in a straight line use a hanging as a door curtain to cause fast-moving Shar Chi or killing breath to slow down and turn auspicious. I place embroidered versions of these eight objects on either side of my front door to welcome in the good Sheng Chi.

referred to as the wheel of life, the wheel of truth, the wheel of a thousand spokes, and the wheel of the cosmos. It symbolizes the noble and wisdom truths of Buddha's teachings. Some say the wheel symbolizes the Buddha himself and that it is the Holy One who drew the wheel with grains of rice taken from the rice field. The spokes of the wheel represent rays of sacred light emanating from the Buddha himself and there can be any number of spokes, from as few as eight to as many as a thousand. The turning of the wheel represents Buddha's doctrines, or dharma, being taught by lineage teachers, called gurus or lamas.

From a Feng Shui perspective, the wheel represents the inner Feng Shui of the mind and overcoming the three poisons of existence. These three poisons are ignorance, anger, and attachment – considered to be the three root causes of human suffering. The wheel thus symbolizes the conquest of suffering by overcoming the three poison arrows that cause these sufferings for human beings.

Placing the wheel symbol in the house signifies obtaining peace of mind and growing in wisdom. It is particularly suitable for those looking for the real meaning of life.

THE JAR

The jar looks like a vase with a cover, not unlike the urn that is used as a receptacle for keeping the relics of ancestors. In the case of the auspicious jar, this is deemed to contain the holy relics of saints and high lamas. These relics are valued highly by Buddhists who regard the jar, as the receptacle for such relics, as an auspicious object. This is a symbol that was also said to have been found on the Buddha's footprints.

I do not view the jar as a Feng Shui object in the sense of it bringing any material advantage. As a Buddhist, I value very highly the relics of Buddhist high lamas and I believe that by keeping them on my altar, huge blessings are bestowed on my household, and my own practice is enormously enhanced. This is based not on Feng Shui but on my own spiritual and religious belief.

Placing a jar like this in the house is therefore not necessarily a Feng Shui recommendation. This symbol is included in this book simply because it is one of the eight auspicious objects of Buddhism. Since Buddhism is widespread in China, all the symbols associated with Buddhist practice have been incorporated into many

A VASE SYMBOLIZES PEACE AND HARMONY, ESPECIALLY WHEN FILLED WITH SUITABLY CHOSEN FLOWERS.

traditional beliefs, one of which is Feng Shui. Understanding the background of objects considered to be auspicious helps you to decide whether or not to place one in your home.

THE VASE

The vase is a symbol of peace and harmony and the placement of flowers in a vase, depending what kind of flowers they are, gives rise to a plethora of rich symbolic meanings (*see* pages 84–87). As one of the eight auspicious Buddhist objects the vase symbolizes a receptacle of the blessings of Buddha – manifested in the form of pure nectar and white light. The vase brings peace of mind and happiness.

From a Feng Shui viewpoint a large vase has several uses. If it is used to contain flowers then it is a good thing to place four season flowers in it and in any combination so as to create peace all year round for the household. The vase can also be transformed into a wealth vase by filling it with symbols of wealth and prosperity. Vases that contain auspicious symbols can be placed anywhere in the house except the kitchen. Ideally also fresh flowers should not be placed in bedrooms.

When you purchase vases and urns it is good to be careful that you do not purchase the variety that is used for keeping the ashes and bones of ancestors. These are seldom made in fine porcelain. Nor will they be made from lacquer or bronze. Instead, they are usually earthenware urns that are at least 2–3ft (60–90cm) high. These are called bone vases and are not suitable for keeping flowers or for making into wealth vases. One way to make sure you don't inadvertently buy one of these vases is to buy one that has an open mouth, rather than one with a cap.

 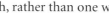

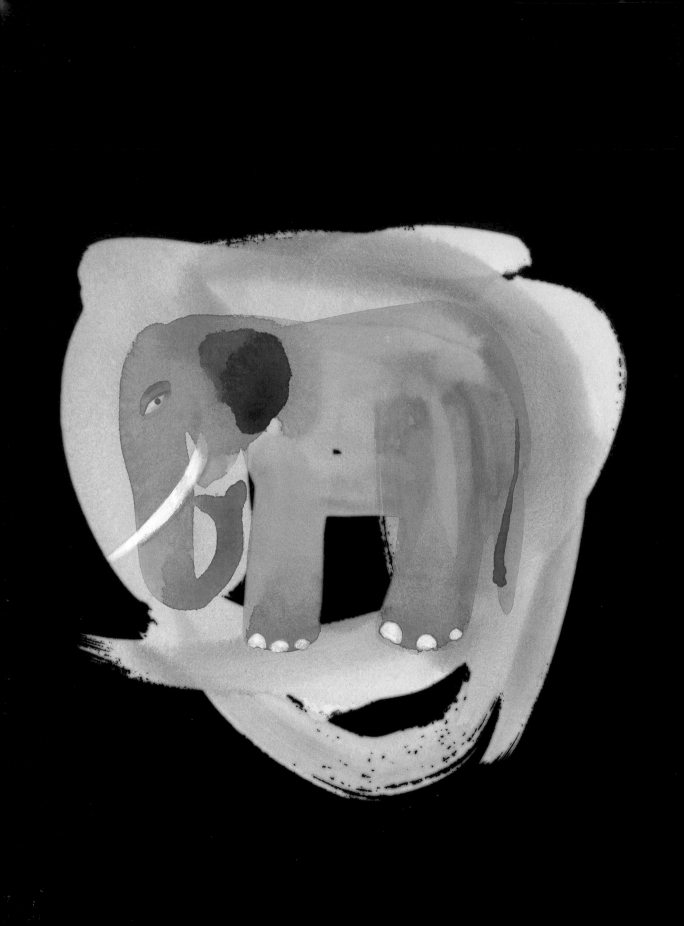

9

THE EIGHT PRECIOUS TREASURES

The eight precious treasures of Feng Shui overlap the eight auspicious objects of the preceding chapter (including the wheel and the vase, see pages 114–115) but under this category they symbolize prosperity and abundance of material possessions. For example, there is the precious jewel that signifies all the manifestations of great wealth. In addition, there is the precious queen, who signifies the powerful matriarch, the precious general, the precious minister, who ensures there is peace and prosperity, the precious horse, and the precious elephant, which brings an abundance of male heirs and good descendants' luck. These eight precious objects are part of the mandala offering contained in Buddhist prayers.

Treasures

Symbols of wealth and prosperity that come from the ground represent manifestations of wealth found in the earth. Thus bright and precious stones – diamonds, crystals, jade – are also powerful symbols of prosperity. These can be displayed on the body, in the home, or in the office to create an abundance of wealth Chi.

THE PRECIOUS JEWEL

The best symbol of the precious jewel is the diamond, and there are beautiful imitations of the diamond fashioned out of reconstituted quartz crystal that can be displayed in the home to attract wealth luck. Feng Shui belief in the efficacy of the jewel comes from its being one of the eight precious treasures said to be mentally created and then included in mandala offerings. The origins of mandala offerings are found in Buddhism and Hinduism, and in many of these temples stunning mandalas made of colored sand are still created for various rituals and puja ceremonies.

Place a crystal jewel, cut and fashioned into the shape of a diamond, on the southwest wall of your hall or bedroom to simulate wealth luck in relationships and in the northeast for wealth luck in your studies and education. Place it in the west or northwest for prosperity and wealth luck.

To the Chinese, the precious jewel is their favorite gemstone – jade – which occurs in all shades from white to green, with the most precious, and hence most valuable, being jade

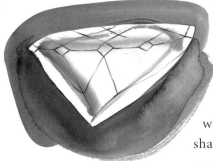

AN IMITATION DIAMOND CAN BE FASHIONED FROM QUARTZ CRYSTAL AND USED TO ATTRACT WEALTH LUCK.

WHEN WORN ON THE BODY, JADE PROTECTS AGAINST ILLNESS AND POOR HEALTH. A RING IS AN EASY WAY TO DO THIS.

of a translucent green color. This jewel is considered to be an extremely lucky object to wear. Because of this, jade has been widely used to decorate belts and headdresses as insignias of high rank. Worn on the body, jade symbolizes protection against illness and poor health. It is also believed to strengthen the physical constitution of anyone wearing it. Thus matriarchs were extremely fond of wearing jade bangles on the hands since this ensured that the cool jade surface would be in constant contact with the skin.

THE PRECIOUS QUEEN

The precious queen epitomizes the essence and spirit of the matriarch. It is a powerful symbol, and hanging pictures of any queen familiar to you always creates good energy Chi for the mother and female members of the family. In Chinese culture, the queen almost always refers to the legendary Taoist Queen of Heaven who is also sometimes referred to as the patron Goddess of Sailors and Sea-going Men because she is believed to ensure good weather and safe conduct for their journeys on the high seas. She is known as Ma Tsu Po.

The precious queen is also part of the Buddhist mandala offering and in this context she can be viewed as the matriarchal equivalent of the emperor. Thus it is considered excellent Feng Shui to display images of matriarchs in the home. The sector to activate is the southwest since this is the place of the trigram kun, which signifies the essence of the matriarchal spirit.

References to the queen can also refer to Hsi Wang Mu – the Queen of the West. Her image in the home is said to bring enormous good fortune (*see* page 53).

THE PRECIOUS GENERAL

Almost all cultures have their military heroes – the equivalent of China's precious generals, the heroes of the Three Kingdoms period. In Feng Shui, the military leader symbolizes the guardian who protects against all the ill winds that blow against the household.

The most famous general in Chinese history is the general Kuan Ti, later known as Kuan Kung and deified as the God of War. Kuan Kung eventually also became the God of Wealth. Thus he wears many hats and is a most useful personage to have in the house. Placing his image in the home, especially when directly facing the front door, ensures that his fierce countenance will scare away any killing breath (*see* page 94).

Those of you who are wary of placing Chinese deities in your home could consider placing the figurine of a military figure that symbolizes bravery, courage, and fearlessness. He can then represent the precious general for you. Military generals on horseback also have good meanings but do not let the horse be pointing directly at the door.

WATCHPOINT

It is believed that negative energy does not dare enter into the presence of the great warrior Kuan Kung.

THE PRECIOUS MINISTER

When a household is well managed there will be harmony and prosperity. The presence of the precious minister implies this state of affairs as well as the following types of luck for the household:

- The family will benefit from a powerful and successful patriarch who is highly regarded in the corridors of power. The precious minister is deemed to be both the benefactor and the patron of the house.
- The family will be wealthy and have the ability to maintain its lifestyle and residence.
- There will always be harmony in the household; and this implies good feelings and loyalty between siblings as well as between the various womenfolk who live under the same roof.

Select figurines that personify attributes and qualities you admire. For example, in my home I have a particularly good ceramic sculpture of Pao Kung – the judge famed for his wisdom of judgments. To me he signifies success with principles. Family patriarchs who have been honored with high awards should display photographs of the patriarch in full regalia in the home.

Pictures taken with ministers are good Feng Shui and these should be prominently displayed in the living room, either on sideboards or on top of the piano. Also, when you display the symbolic presence of powerful men (and women) in your house, the badge of power and success permeates the environment in a positive way.

THE PRECIOUS HORSE

The horse is the seventh creature of the Chinese zodiac. In Buddhist texts it stands for endurance, loyalty, and purity. It is precious when it is depicted laden with precious things. Then it expresses the aspiration of a comfortable life and the attainment of high rank, which brings recognition and a life of comfort.

The tribute horse is an auspicious variation of this same idea (*see* pages 43–44). In Feng Shui, the horse symbolizes Yang energy and its representative direction on the zodiac is the south. When you wish to activate fully the energies of the south one of the best ways of doing so is to place a tribute horse or a precious horse in that corner of the house. This is especially helpful for those people wanting to do well in their careers, particularly those who want their talents and hard work to be recognized by the right people.

THE HORSE, ESPECIALLY WHEN LADEN WITH PRECIOUS THINGS, SYMBOLIZES A COMFORTABLE LIFE AND PROMOTION IN THE WORK PLACE.

THE PRECIOUS ELEPHANT

The elephant is one of the precious holy animals of Buddhism, and in Thailand, the precious elephant has always been strongly associated with the country's image. In Burma too, the elephant is accorded special status. Buddha is said to have been conceived by entering his mother's side as a white elephant, and thus till this day, sightings of white elephants are always regarded as a good luck omen. Meanwhile, according to Hindu mythology, the world is believed to be resting on the back of an elephant who stands atop a tortoise, and one of the most powerful and popular Gods of Hinduism, the Lord Ganesh, is depicted as an elephant.

Mahayana Buddhists of China frequently represent the elephant with a lotus flower on its back upon which is seated the Buddha of Wisdom, known as Pu Hsien Pu Sart in Chinese and the Buddha Manjushuri in Tibetan. The precious elephant is also regarded as the bearer of the wish-granting jewel as well as the sacred begging bowl of the Buddha. The Thais have adopted the white elephant as the country's national symbol, believing it to be an emanation of a future Buddha.

In Asia, therefore, the elephant is accorded divine status, and those Buddhists belonging to the older generation even consider it a symbol of universal sovereignty. There is something infinitely good and benign about the elephant image. Many people place miniature images on their altar as an offering to Buddha believing it to symbolize many good things.

If you wish to display the precious elephant in your home as a symbol of good fortune, it is a good idea to place a basket of precious things on its back since this denotes the elephant bringing these auspicious objects into the home. Also place a pair of elephants near the vicinity of the front door either inside or outside the home (*see also* page 44). You can place flowering plants or anything else deemed auspicious on top of the elephant. He is said to have the strength and energy to hold up the world.

FOR GOOD FORTUNE, PLACE AN ELEPHANT ON EACH SIDE OF YOUR MAIN DOOR.

THE MANDALA

Placing a mandala in your home is said to be most auspicious. Buddhists of the Mahayana tradition create mandalas whenever there is a particularly important puja being conducted or when a special initiation is being done. For instance, whenever His Holiness the Dalai Lama does an initiation after a teaching, his monks and disciples usually construct an appropriate mandala as an offering.

Making the mandala requires skill and craftsmanship. The best mandala makers are monks from India, Nepal, and Tibet. The mandala is usually built on a base that has been blessed with incense and fragrance. In the center is placed the symbolic Mount Meru, the Buddhist paradise mountain, said to be the center of the world. A mandala signifies a pure universe where all manner of precious things are placed together as a special offering to the Buddhas. In this way, the mandala simulates the central mountain, the four continents, all manner of precious things, the sun and the moon, the precious parasol, and the banner of victory. It is not surprising, then, that it is so auspicious.

Many other cultural traditions refer to a central mountain deemed to be the holy mountain, and in Feng Shui, mountains play a large part in bringing good Chi flows to homes located in auspicious orientation to them.

USING THE MAGIC OF THE WINDS

A famous Taoist master from Hong Kong once gave me a wish list ritual, which he said would enhance my business luck. The ritual was that I was to write down whatever I wanted really badly – onto a helium-filled balloon. I was to write my wish clearly and succinctly and then I was to release the balloon and let it fly up high into the sky. It wasn't Feng Shui by any means – it was a mind ritual that just seemed to be such fun to do. One

A MANDALA IS A MOST PRECIOUS ITEM
THAT REQUIRES GREAT CRAFTSMANSHIP
IN ITS MAKING.

THE RITUAL OF WRITING A WISH
ON A HELIUM-FILLED BALLOON
IS BELIEVED TO BRING YOU
YOUR HEART'S DESIRE.

Sunday I wrote down my wish to be able to shop like a queen in all the capitals of the world. I wanted to close a business deal for myself that would enable me to love my work. I was fed up of being a banker. I wanted to do something fun, something more feminine. So I wished for a department store. That was how I won a deal that enabled me to have my own chain of department stores – and allowed me to shop like an empress for two years when I was the stores' executive chairman. Talk about having one's wishes come true. During those years I shopped in all the fashion capitals of the world. I shopped for my chain of stores. I shopped till I dropped.

A variation of the balloon wish list is the banner of victory that you can tie across your garden. Let the winds carry your wishes up into the sky so they can be actualized for you.

10

THE TWELVE ANIMALS OF THE ZODIAC

The lunar year in which you were born plays a significant part in your own personal Feng Shui. Once you know your animal sign you can select the symbols that are auspicious for you and place them in specific locations in the home to bring excellent fortune. There will also be years when you will need to protect yourself from the negative Chi created by the Five Yellow, the Three Killings, or the Grand Duke Jupiter. In the following pages you will discover how to use your animal sign and its corresponding element as powerful symbols of good fortune and protection.

The Chinese Zodiac

Chinese astrology has little to do with the sun, moon, or stars. Unlike Western astrology, it does not look heavenward to chart the movement of the constellations or predict destiny; it is about the understanding of the fundamentals of the astrological and divinitive sciences, such as the five elements, Yin and Yang, and the Chinese cycles of time.

THE TWELVE ANIMALS

The 12 animals of the Chinese zodiac symbolize the earthly branches. Each of the animals, starting with the rat and ending with the pig, has a corresponding compass direction, which offers specific guidelines on where to place images of these animals to magnify their energy and symbolic attributes. The direction of each animal sign also offers vital clues on the "danger" sectors in the home in each year.

Take note of the Flying Star Feng Shui taboos in each year, and note how they affect each of the animal signs. The table below is very valuable because it summarizes where the three danger sectors are for each year. These are sectors that are occupied by the deadly Five Yellow, the Three Killings, and the Grand Duke Jupiter. The text that follows gives specific symbolic Feng Shui solutions for each year's taboo sectors for every animal sign. Study this chapter carefully.

DANGER SECTORS BY LUNAR YEAR

YEAR	ANIMAL SIGN OR EARTHLY BRANCH	PLACE OF THE FIVE YELLOW (90 DEGREES)	PLACE OF THE THREE KILLINGS (45 DEGREES)	PLACE OF THE GRAND DUKE JUPITER (15 DEGREES)
2000	Dragon	North	South	East-southeast
2001	Snake	Southwest	East	South-southeast
2002	Horse	East	North	South
2003	Sheep	Southeast	West	South-southwest
2004	Monkey	Center	South	West-southwest
2005	Rooster	Northwest	East	West
2006	Dog	West	North	West-northwest
2007	Boar	Northeast	West	North-northwest
2008	Rat	South	South	North
2009	Ox	North	East	North-northeast
2010	Tiger	Southwest	North	East-northeast
2011	Rabbit	South	West	East

THE LUNAR CALENDAR

Please refer to the 100-year lunar calendar overleaf to determine your heavenly stem element and your earthly branch animal sign and element. The Chinese calendar is made up of 60-year cycles that are differentiated according to heavenly stems and earthly branches. There are 10 stems and 12 branches. In the 60-year cycle the stems comprise the five elements with a Yin or a Yang aspect (hence 5 x 2 = 10 stems). The 12 stems refer to the animal signs.

This system of stems and branches comprehensively symbolizes the interaction between heaven and earthly forces. The stems and branches also reflect and determine the destiny of humankind. Thus all divination and fortune-telling methods ultimately rely on the correct interpretations of the personal stems and branches of any individual. These stems and branches can also be used to personalize the Feng Shui of any individual, and this section of the book directly addresses this.

Using the 100-year lunar calendar overleaf you can figure out your heavenly stem in your year of birth and your animal sign and its corresponding element (earthly branch). From your earthly branch you will be able to select the symbols that are auspicious for

TAKING COMPASS DIRECTIONS

It is useful to learn how to take compass directions from the center of the house. Mark out the compass sector that corresponds to your animal sign to the exact degree. Each animal sign is said to occupy 30 degrees of the compass total of 360 degrees. Learn to mark out the sector that represents your animal sign in your house. If you do not know how to read a compass, get someone to teach you before attempting to do it yourself. Invest in a good compass. Any Western-style compass is fine. Do not flip or reverse the directions when applying them.

you. Next, by referring to the text about each animal on pages 128–139 you will be able to identify the specific location in the home to place these symbols.

Note that the years listed with each animal's description have not been adjusted to take account of the lunar New Year. Thus if you were born in the month of January 1960, the chances are that you do not belong to the rat year but instead to the previous year, which is the year of the boar. In the same way, you could still be a rat if you were born in the January of the following year. To check your date of birth against the lunar calendar refer to the 100-year lunar calendar, when the relevant dates are given for each new lunar year.

LOCATING THE AREA OF
YOUR HOME THAT PERTAINS TO
YOUR ANIMAL OF THE ZODIAC
REQUIRES A COMPASS READING.

THE CHINESE 100-YEAR CALENDAR:
1912 TO 1962

Western Calendar Dates	Animal Sign	Earthly Branch Element	Heavenly Stem Element
18 Feb 1912 – 5 Feb 1913	Rat	water	water
6 Feb 1913 – 25 Jan 1914	Ox	earth	water
26 Jan 1914 – 13 Feb 1915	Tiger	wood	wood
14 Feb 1915 – 2 Feb 1916	Rabbit	wood	wood
3 Feb 1916 – 22 Jan 1917	Dragon	earth	fire
23 Jan 1917 – 10 Feb 1918	Snake	fire	fire
11 Feb 1918 – 31 Jan 1919	Horse	fire	earth
1 Feb 1919 – 19 Feb 1920	Sheep	earth	earth
20 Feb 1920 – 7 Feb 1921	Monkey	metal	metal
8 Feb 1921 – 27 Jan 1922	Rooster	metal	metal
28 Jan 1922 – 15 Feb 1923	Dog	earth	water
16 Feb 1923 – 4 Feb 1924	Boar	water	water

START OF 60-YEAR CYCLE

Western Calendar Dates	Animal Sign	Earthly Branch Element	Heavenly Stem Element
5 Feb 1924 – 23 Jan 1925	Rat	water	wood
24 Jan 1925 – 12 Feb 1926	Ox	earth	wood
13 Feb 1926 – 1 Feb 1927	Tiger	wood	fire
2 Feb 1927 – 22 Jan 1928	Rabbit	wood	fire
23 Jan 1928 – 9 Feb 1929	Dragon	earth	earth
10 Feb 1929 – 29 Jan 1930	Snake	fire	earth
30 Jan 1930 – 16 Feb 1931	Horse	fire	metal
17 Feb 1931 – 5 Feb 1932	Sheep	earth	metal
6 Feb 1932 – 25 Jan 1933	Monkey	metal	water
26 Jan 1933 – 13 Feb 1934	Rooster	metal	water
14 Feb 1934 – 3 Feb 1935	Dog	earth	wood

Western Calendar Dates	Animal Sign	Earthly Branch Element	Heavenly Stem Element
4 Feb 1935 – 23 Jan 1936	Boar	water	wood
24 Jan 1936 – 10 Feb 1937	Rat	water	fire
11 Feb 1937 – 30 Jan 1938	Ox	earth	fire
31 Jan 1938 – 18 Feb 1939	Tiger	wood	earth
19 Feb 1939 – 7 Feb 1940	Rabbit	wood	earth
8 Feb 1940 – 26 Jan 1941	Dragon	earth	metal
27 Jan 1941 – 14 Feb 1942	Snake	metal	metal
15 Feb 1942 – 4 Feb 1943	Horse	metal	water
5 Feb 1943 – 24 Jan 1944	Sheep	earth	water
25 Jan 1944 – 12 Feb 1945	Monkey	metal	wood
13 Feb 1945 – 1 Feb 1946	Rooster	metal	wood
2 Feb 1946 – 21 Jan 1947	Dog	earth	fire
22 Jan 1947 – 9 Feb 1948	Boar	water	fire
10 Feb 1948 – 28 Jan 1949	Rat	water	earth
29 Jan 1949 – 16 Feb 1950	Ox	earth	earth
17 Feb 1950 – 5 Feb 1951	Tiger	wood	metal
6 Feb 1951 – 26 Jan 1952	Rabbit	wood	metal
27 Jan 1952 – 13 Feb 1953	Dragon	earth	water
14 Feb 1953 – 2 Feb 1954	Snake	fire	water
3 Feb 1954 – 23 Jan 1955	Horse	fire	wood
24 Jan 1955 – 11 Feb 1956	Sheep	earth	wood
12 Feb 1956 – 30 Jan 1957	Monkey	metal	fire
31 Jan 1957 – 17 Feb 1958	Rooster	metal	fire
18 Feb 1958 – 7 Feb 1959	Dog	earth	earth
8 Feb 1959 – 27 Jan 1960	Boar	water	earth
28 Jan 1960 – 14 Feb 1961	Rat	water	metal
15 Feb 1961 – 4 Feb 1962	Ox	earth	metal

THE CHINESE 100-YEAR CALENDAR: 1962 TO 2008

Western Calendar Dates	Animal Sign	Earthly Branch Element	Heavenly Stem Element	Western Calendar Dates	Animal Sign	Earthly Branch Element	Heavenly Stem Element
5 Feb 1962 – 24 Jan 1963	Tiger	wood	water	20 Feb 1985 – 8 Feb 1986	Ox	earth	wood
25 Jan 1963 – 12 Feb 1964	Rabbit	wood	water	9 Feb 1986 – 28 Jan 1987	Tiger	wood	fire
13 Feb 1964 – 1 Feb 1965	Dragon	earth	wood	29 Jan 1987 – 16 Feb 1988	Rabbit	wood	fire
2 Feb 1965 – 20 Jan 1966	Snake	fire	wood	17 Feb 1988 – 5 Feb 1989	Dragon	earth	earth
21 Jan 1966 – 8 Feb 1967	Horse	fire	fire	6 Feb 1989 – 26 Jan 1990	Snake	fire	earth
9 Feb 1967 – 29 Jan 1968	Sheep	earth	fire	27 Jan 1990 – 14 Feb 1991	Horse	fire	metal
30 Jan 1968 – 16 Feb 1969	Monkey	metal	earth	15 Feb 1991 – 3 Feb 1992	Sheep	earth	metal
17 Feb 1969 – 5 Feb 1970	Rooster	metal	earth	4 Feb 1992 – 22 Jan 1993	Monkey	metal	water
6 Feb 1970 – 26 Jan 1971	Dog	earth	metal	23 Jan 1993 – 9 Feb 1994	Rooster	metal	water
27 Jan 1971 – 14 Feb 1972	Boar	water	metal	10 Feb 1994 – 30 Jan 1995	Dog	earth	wood
15 Feb 1972 – 2 Feb 1973	Rat	water	water	31 Jan 1995 – 18 Feb 1996	Boar	water	wood
3 Feb 1973 22 Jan 1974	Ox	earth	water	19 Feb 1996 – 6 Feb 1997	Rat	water	fire
23 Jan 1974 – 10 Feb 1975	Tiger	wood	wood	7 Feb 1997 – 27 Jan 1998	Ox	earth	fire
11 Feb 1975 – 30 Jan 1976	Rabbit	wood	wood	28 Jan 1998 –15 Feb 1999	Tiger	wood	earth
31 Jan 1976 – 17 Feb 1977	Dragon	earth	fire	16 Feb 1999 – 4 Feb 2000	Rabbit	wood	earth
18 Feb 1977 – 6 Feb 1978	Snake	fire	fire	5 Feb 2000 – 23 Jan 2001	Dragon	earth	metal
7 Feb 1978 – 27 Jan 1979	Horse	fire	earth	24 Jan 2001 – 11 Feb 2002	Snake	fire	metal
28 Jan 1979 – 15 Feb 1980	Sheep	earth	earth	12 Feb 2002 – 31 Jan 2003	Horse	fire	water
16 Feb 1980 – 4 Feb 1981	Monkey	metal	metal	1 Feb 2003 – 21 Jan 2004	Sheep	earth	water
5 Feb 1981 – 24 Jan 1982	Rooster	metal	metal	22 Jan 2004 8 Feb 2005	Monkey	metal	wood
25 Jan 1982 – 12 Feb 1983	Dog	earth	water	9 Feb 2005 – 28 Jan 2006	Rooster	metal	wood
13 Feb 1983 – 1 Feb 1984	Boar	water	water	29 Jan 2006 – 17 Feb 2007	Dog	earth	fire
2 Feb 1984 – 19 Feb 1985	Rat	water	wood	18 Feb 2007 – 6 Feb 2008	Boar	water	fire

THE RAT

The rat is the first sign of the Chinese zodiac.

Years
1912, 1924, 1936, 1948,
1960, 1972, 1984, 1996

Element
water

Hour
between 11 p.m. and 1 a.m.

Compass direction
between 337.5 and 7.5 degrees – north

Good luck sector
north

To energize good wealth luck in your good luck sector there are several symbolic things you can do:

• Place the metaphorical precious mongoose that looks like a rat in the sector of your house that lies between the degrees indicated above, or put any kind of image of the rat in this part of the house.

• Activate the same sector with a water feature since this is the intrinsic element of your animal sign. It would, however, be quite bad luck if your sector (north) were afflicted with a toilet or a kitchen since this would cause your personalized sector to become negatively affected.

• Two other sectors deemed excellent for you correspond to the animal years of the dragon and the monkey. The direction of the dragon is east-southeast and the direction of the monkey is west-southwest.

Those born in the year of the rat are advised to observe the following ideas to improve their luck:

In the years of the dragon (2000) the rat enjoys excellent fortunes. Your wealth luck will be even better if you display dragon images. A phoenix in the south will bring recognition and honors. Place a five-rod wind chime in the north.

In the years of the snake (2001) the rat continues with his good fortunes. Add a couple of fu dogs or *chi lins* to ensure there is no serious loss of money due to your being too trusting. Place a wealth plant and a water feature in the southwest.

In the years of the horse (2002) the rat faces financial difficulties and the possibility of lawsuits and family problems. To counteract this, hang a wind chime or place fu dogs and amulets in the east for protection and to guard against the Five Yellow here this year. Light up the south with a chandelier to appease the Grand Duke.

In the years of the sheep (2003) the rat's fortunes recover and are poised for growth. Place a three-legged toad or coins to enhance further prosperity luck.

The years of the monkey (2004) are other good years when the rat enjoys a continued spate of good fortune. Place dragon images to enhance the luck.

The years of the rooster (2005) are great for business. Hang wind chimes in the west and bring in Sau, the God of Longevity, to protect from fatigue and overworking.

The years of the dog (2006) are not good so the rat needs to lie low. This is a year when you require protection. Place bells and wind chimes in the west to keep the Five Yellow under control. Also bring back the amulets and the tortoise.

In the years of the boar (2007) again try to stay cool and lie low.

THE OX

The ox is the second sign of the Chinese zodiac.

Years
1913, 1925, 1937, 1949,
1961, 1973, 1985, 1997

Element
earth

Hour
between 1 and 3 a.m.

Compass direction
between 7.5 and 37.5 degrees – north-northeast

Good luck sector
north – northeast

To energize good wealth luck in your good luck sector there are several symbolic things you can do:

• Place the symbolic wish-fulfilling cow in the sector of your home that lies between the degrees indicated above, or you can use any image of a cow, bull, or anything belonging to this family in this part of the house. The best images would be made of ceramic, crystal, or other material that belongs to the earth element.

• Activate the same sector with any earth element feature since this is the intrinsic element of your animal sign. It would, however, be quite bad luck if your sector (north-northeast) were afflicted with a toilet or a kitchen since this would cause your personalized sector to become negatively affected.

• Two other sectors deemed excellent for you correspond to the animal years of the snake and rooster. The direction of the snake is south-southeast and the direction of the rooster is west. Those born in the year of the ox are advised to observe the following ideas to improve their luck:

The years of the dragon (2000) are mixed. The ox benefits greatly if a *ru yi* is placed in the office or at work to enhance authority. Protect against the Five Yellow in the north with a wind chime that is made from metal and features hollow rods.

In the years of the snake (2001) the ox enters a good period. Let money luck flow in. Get a money or gem tree because this magnifies your good luck.

The years of the horse (2002) are unsettling times. Emotional and family problems prevail. Counter this by placing crystals and mandarin ducks in the southwest of your bedroom. Amulets and the dragon tortoise also help. Hang a wind chime in the east to control the Five Yellow and place a Laughing Buddha in the south to appease the Grand Duke Jupiter.

In the years of the sheep (2003) confidence levels increase. Place bright red lights in the south and display the Fuk Luk Sau in the dining room.

The years of the monkey (2004) are abundant with good fortune. Place the coins, three-legged toads, and the dragon phoenix in the living room. Energize!

In the years of the rooster (2005) good fortune times continue. Enhance with six- or seven-rod wind chimes in the west or northwest.

The years of the dog (2006) are not good. It is time to lie low and you will benefit from protection symbols. Place fu dogs in front of the house and wind chimes in the west.

The years of the boar (2007) are very busy. Enhance work luck by energizing the north with fish in a pond.

THE TIGER

The tiger is the third sign of the Chinese zodiac.

Years	Hour
1914, 1926, 1938, 1950, 1962, 1974, 1986, 1998	between 3 and 5 a.m.

Element
wood

Compass direction
between 37.5 and 67.5 degrees – east-northeast

Good luck sector
east-northeast

To energize good wealth luck in your good luck sector there are several symbolic things you can do:

• Place images of the tiger in the sector of your house that lies between the degrees indicated above. Since your animal sign is that of the tiger you will definitely benefit from the tiger image. To enhance its intrinsic energy, display wooden carvings or sculptures of the tiger. This energizes the wood element and is beneficial.

• Activate the same sector with any wood element feature since this is the intrinsic element of your animal sign. It will, however, be bad luck if your sector (east-northeast) is afflicted with a toilet or a kitchen since this would cause your personalized sector to become negatively affected.

• Two other sectors deemed excellent for you correspond to the animal years of the horse and the dog. The direction of the horse is south and the direction of the dog is west-northwest. Those born in the year of the tiger are advised to observe the following ideas to improve their luck:

In the years of the dragon (2000) there is a slight reversal of fortunes. Protect with protective door images or a pair of fu dogs, one on each side of the door as explained on page 93. Also place seven-rod wind chimes in the west to enhance the tiger's intrinsic Chi.

The years of the snake (2001) are a quiet time for the tiger, because luck is moderate. Install water features in the north to help you relax.

The years of the horse (2002) are exceptionally good. Place lots of Feng Shui enhancers – coins, arrowanas, dragons, and tortoises – to magnify good luck.

In the years of the sheep (2003) the tiger extends his run of good luck. Continue with the Feng Shui energizers and add a water feature in the north or southeast.

The years of the monkey (2004) will be times of disappointments and setbacks when the tiger must be protected from hostile forces. During this time protect against the Grand Duke by placing a crystal chandelier in the west-southwest sector of your home.

The years of the rooster (2005) are mixed, with the second half being better. Place wind chimes in the northwest and a three-legged toad near the front door.

In the years of the dog (2006) the tiger benefits from help and support from powerful patrons. Energize the northwest with a six-rod wind chime.

In the years of the boar (2007) there is plenty of money luck. Enhance this with coins and fish features otherwise it dissipates in the second half of the year.

THE RABBIT

The rabbit is the fourth sign of the Chinese zodiac.

Years
1915, 1927, 1939, 1951,
1963, 1975, 1987, 1999

Element
wood

Hour
between 5 and 7 a.m.

Compass direction
between 67.5 and 97.5 degrees – east

Good luck sector
east

To energize good wealth luck in your good luck sector there are several symbolic things you can do:

• Place images of the rabbit in the sector of your house that lies between the degrees indicated above. To enhance its intrinsic energy, display wooden carvings or sculptures of the rabbit. Keep rabbits in pairs rather than singly.

• Activate the same sector with any wood element feature since this is the intrinsic element of your animal sign. It will, however, be bad luck for you if this sector (east) is afflicted with a toilet or a kitchen since this would cause your personalized sector to become negatively affected.

• Two other sectors deemed excellent for you correspond to the animal years of the sheep and the boar. The direction of the sheep is south-southwest and the boar is north-northwest.

Those born in the year of the rabbit are advised to observe the following ideas to improve their luck:

In the years of the dragon (2000) the rabbit can look forward to a very good year. Place coins tied with red thread in the southeast and move the three-legged toad to the southeast of the living room to attract prosperity.

In the years of the snake (2001) protect against the problems of this year by placing a deer in the northwest of the living room. You must have wind chimes in the southwest this year.

In the years of the horse (2002) good friends rally around to help. Energize the southwest with crystals. Also a pair of rhinoceroses in the living room helps.

In the years of the sheep (2003) this is the time to place a gem tree in your living room. Look for one that is filled with yellow and red-colored semiprecious stones and is at least 10in (25cm) tall. Place it in the southeast or south of your living room.

In the years of the monkey (2004) it is a good time to consolidate. Place the dragon tortoise to bring you stability, harmony, and protection.

The years of the rooster (2005) is a dangerous period when financial losses could prove disastrous. You must have the *chi lin* or a pair of fu dogs, and special amulets hung up near the entrance door will also help. Hang a crystal chandelier in the west to appease the Grand Duke or hang a seven-rod wind chime.

In the years of the dog (2006) obstacles remain. Place a mother and child rhinoceros and a three-legged toad in the living room to overcome money problems.

The years of the boar (2007) are mixed. Place three sheep standing on coins to overcome troublemakers in your life. Also place fu dogs at your gate.

THE DRAGON

The dragon is the fifth sign of the Chinese zodiac.

Years
1916, 1928, 1940, 1952, 1964, 1976, 1988, 2000

Element
earth

Hour
between 7 and 9 a.m.

Compass direction
between 97.5 and 127.5 degrees – east-southeast

Good luck sector
east-southeast

To energize good wealth luck in your good luck sector there are things you can do to energize your animal sign:

• Place images of the dragon in the sector of your house that lies between the degrees indicated above. To enhance its intrinsic energy, display dragons made from earth materials such as ceramics, porcelain, crystal, and so forth.

• Activate the same sector with any earth element feature since this is the intrinsic element of your animal sign. It will, however, be bad luck for you if this sector (east-southeast) is afflicted with a toilet or a kitchen since this would cause your personalized sector to become badly affected.

• Two other sectors deemed excellent for those born in dragon years are those that correspond to the animal years of the monkey and rat. The direction of the monkey is west-southwest and the direction of the rat is north.

Dragon year people are advised to observe the following:

In the years of the dragon (2000) there is good fortune when everything becomes successful. Place dragon images in the east and southeast of the home to enhance the good fortune.

In the years of the snake (2001) everything continues to go smoothly. You will benefit from water features in the north and from placing the gem tree in the east. Crystals in the southwest enhance relationship luck.

The years of the horse (2002) are moderate years for the dragon. Place images of the phoenix or its substitutes (peacock or rooster) in the south to clarify uncertain luck. Wind chimes in the west bring good luck, and are important in the east to control the Five Yellow.

In the years of the sheep (2003) there are mixed signals. Enhance career luck with a water feature in the north and place a *pik yao* on your desk to overcome obstacles. Place Sau, the God of Longevity, to overcome health problems.

In the years of the monkey (2004) business achieves good performance. For luck, place a sailing ship facing inward and, if possible, facing the northeast direction.

The years of the rooster (2005) are very auspicious for the dragon. Place a three-legged toad near the front door and a seven-rod wind chime in the west. This is a good year to proceed with any new ventures. It is a good year to take risks.

The years of the dog (2006) will be the dragon's worst time so be careful. Definitely get a pair of *chi lin* and fu dogs to flank your entrance, and a Laughing Buddha and wind chimes for the west to control the deadly Five Yellow.

In the years of the boar (2007) place the dragon tortoise in the north to help you get out of last year's bad period. Light up the south for recognition luck.

THE SNAKE

The snake is the sixth sign of the Chinese zodiac.

Years
1917, 1929, 1941, 1953,
1965, 1977, 1989, 2001

Element
fire

Hour
between 9 and 11 a.m.

Compass direction
between 127.5 and 157.5 degrees – south-southeast

Good luck sector
south-southeast

To energize good wealth luck in your good luck sector there are several symbolic things you might want to consider doing:

• Place images of the snake in the sector of your house that lies between the degrees indicated above. To enhance its intrinsic energy, display the snake image in a red color – choose images made from wood since this element produces fire.

• Activate the same sector with any fire element feature since this is the intrinsic element of your animal sign. Thus keep this sector brightly lit. It will be bad luck for you if this sector (south-southeast) is afflicted with a toilet or a kitchen.

• For those born in snake years, sectors that correspond to the animal years of the rooster and the ox are also deemed excellent for them. The direction of the rooster is west and the direction of the ox is north-northeast.

Snake year people are advised to observe the following:

In the years of the dragon (2000) hard times abound. You will need the Lo Shu dragon tortoise amulet to be protected from gossip and losses. Hang wind chimes in the north to control the deadly Five Yellow, and display a horse image in the south to ensure better luck at the end of the year.

In the years of the snake (2001) plans for the future take shape. Place the three-legged toad in your bedroom or near the entrance of your home.

The years of the horse (2002) are good when energizing the south with lights, with the phoenix image, and with the color red. Together they bring excellent fortune.

In the years of the sheep (2003) it is good to activate the luck of the northwest corner with a six-rod wind chime. This brings powerful friends and patrons into your life.

In the years of the monkey (2004) powerful friends bring opportunities and good fortune. Place crystals in the southwest. Display the Fuk Luk Sau in the northwest.

The years of the rooster (2005) are excellent. Activate the luck of the northwest with a six-rod wind chime and the west with a golden deer. Place the *ru yi* on your desk to energize your career luck.

In the years of the dog (2006) there will be good romance and travel luck. Place the conch on your desk and the double happiness sign in your bedroom.

In the years of the boar (2007) display paintings of longevity symbols such as the bamboo and the pine. Overcome health worries with Sau, the God of Longevity, and place wind chimes in the northeast to control the deadly Five Yellow. Finally, do not sit facing the north-northwest this year because you will be confronting the Grand Duke. Instead, place a water feature here.

THE HORSE

The horse is the seventh sign of the Chinese zodiac.

Years
1918, 1930, 1942, 1954,
1966, 1978, 1990, 2002

Element
fire

Hour
between 11 a.m. and 1 p.m.

Compass direction
between 157.5 and 187.5 degrees – south

Good luck sector
south

To energize good wealth luck in your good luck sector there are several symbolic things you can do:

• Place images of the horse in the sector of your home that lies between the degrees indicated above. To enhance its intrinsic energy, display the horse image in whites and reds – Yang colors – and choose images made from wood since this element produces fire.

• Activate the same sector with any fire element feature since this is the intrinsic element of your animal sign. Thus keep this sector brightly lit. It will be bad luck for you if this sector (south) is where a toilet or the kitchen is located since this would cause your personalized sector to be seriously afflicted.

• For those born in horse years, sectors that correspond to the animal years of the dog and the tiger are also deemed excellent. The direction of the dog is west-northwest and the direction of the tiger is east-northeast.

Horse year people are advised to observe the following:

The years of the dragon (2000) are depressing years of uncertainty. But displaying the dragon image in the east and the tortoise image in the north can easily energize good luck.

In the years of the snake (2001) hard work bears fruit when you place the horse image in the south. But also display wind chimes in the west for protection against betrayal.

The years of the horse (2002) are good years, which can be enhanced with all the good fortune symbols of prosperity. Chinese coins will be especially effective for the west and northwest. Tie nine red coins with red thread and hang them on these walls.

In the years of the sheep (2003) place a three-legged toad for continued money luck.

In the years of the monkey (2004) travel luck is good. Place a pair of precious elephants near the front door and a shell (conch) on the coffee table.

The years of the rooster (2005) are moderate years. Display pictures of children with fish in the west and place a water feature in the southeast.

The years of the dog (2006) are good times for college graduates. Place the *ru yi* on your desk and crystals in the northeast to activate the luck of personal growth.

In the years of the boar (2007) you will be confronted with unexpected difficulties and obstacles. Display fu dogs by your entrance door; these will help to press down on any hostile Chi. Do not sit facing north-northwest because this confronts the Grand Duke, which will make a difficult situation even worse. Place wind chimes in the northeast to diffuse negative energy.

THE SHEEP

The sheep is the eighth sign of the Chinese zodiac.

Years
1919, 1931, 1943, 1955,
1967, 1979, 1991, 2003

Element
earth

Hour
between 1 and 3 p.m.

Compass direction
between 187.5 and 217.5 degrees – south-southwest

Good luck sector
south-southwest

To energize good wealth luck in your good luck sector there are several symbolic things you can do:

• Place images of the sheep or goat in the sector of your house that lies between the degrees indicated above. In order to enhance its intrinsic energy, display the sheep image in earth element materials.

• Activate the same sector with the fire element since fire produces earth. The sector will also benefit from porcelain and other decorative ceramic ware.

• For those born in sheep years, there are two other sectors that are also deemed most excellent. These are sectors that correspond to the animal years of the boar and the rabbit. The sector that is identified with the boar is north-northwest and the sector of the rabbit is the east.

Sheep year people are advised to observe the following ideas to improve their luck:

The years of the dragon (2000) are sobering times when the presence of the rhinoceros or the three goats standing on a bed of coins will be of great help. It is also a good time to invite in the Laughing Buddha. Put him in the north this year to overcome the problems of the Five Yellow.

In the years of the snake (2001) the sheep's confidence returns. Place the wish-fulfilling cow in the living room.

The years of the horse (2002) are serene when money luck improves considerably. Place Chinese coins and the auspicious three-legged toad anywhere in the living room but looking at the front door.

The years of the sheep (2003) are a period of good social luck. Relationships bring joy. Place the double happiness symbol and good fortune calligraphy in the living room. For marriage happiness, have images depicting a pair of geese in the bedroom.

The years of the monkey (2004) are a good time to further your career. Introduce a water feature into the north of your living room and keep nine goldfish.

In the years of the rooster (2005) conflicts and hostilities abound. It is best to bring in two fu dogs and a tortoise for protection. Place crystal balls in the southwest to protect against hostility of friends and colleagues.

In the years of the dog (2006) there will be some major setbacks. Place strong Taoist amulets to temper bad luck. Also display the dragon horse or *chi lin*.

In the years of the boar (2007) place a six-rod wind chime in the northwest corner of your living room and bring in the Laughing Buddha and place him in the northeast to absorb problems that are coming your way.

THE MONKEY

The monkey is the ninth sign of the Chinese zodiac.

Years
1920, 1932, 1944, 1956,
1968, 1980, 1992, 2004

Element
metal

Hour
between 3 and 5 p.m.

Compass direction
between 217.5 and 247.5 degrees – west-southwest

Good luck sector
west-southwest

To energize good wealth luck in your good luck sector there are several symbolic things you can do:

• Place images of the monkey in the sector of your house that lies between the compass directions indicated above. In order to enhance its intrinsic energy, display the auspicious Monkey God with peaches. This scene is also painted onto ceramics or porcelain.

• Activate the same sector with any metal element feature since this is the intrinsic element of your animal sign. Thus bells and wind chimes are suitable for this sector. It will be bad luck for you if a toilet or the kitchen is located in this sector (west-southwest) since this would cause your personalized sector to be badly affected.

• Those born in monkey years will also benefit from good symbols placed in sectors that correspond to rat years and dragon years. The sector of the rat is north and that of the dragon is east-southeast.

Monkey year people are advised to observe the following ideas to improve their luck:

In the years of the dragon (2000) fortunes improve considerably. A horse in the south brings recognition luck, and a three-legged toad in the office and living room brings money-making opportunities.

In the years of the snake (2001) powerful mentors come into your life. Energize the northwest with a six-rod windchime and a wealth vase.

In the years of the horse (2002) display the God of Wealth in the southeast. Place the *ru yi* on your desk. Energize the south with bright lights.

In the years of the sheep (2003) enhance travel luck with the conch on your office desk. Display the ten emperor coins behind you at work.

The years of the monkey (2004) will have excellent gains. Place a gem tree in the east and the wish-fulfilling cow in the living room.

In the years of the rooster (2005) there will be good luck when helpful people enhance your good fortune. Place six crystal balls in the northwest for harmony.

In the years of the dog (2006) caution is the watchword. Place fu dogs by the entrance. A pair of *chi lin* at your desk protects against office politics. Control the Five Yellow in the west with wind chimes.

In the years of the boar (2007) you require Taoist amulets to protect you against lawsuits and legal entanglements. Make sure you have the Laughing Buddha in your living room. Place him in the northeast to overcome the deadly Five Yellow.

THE ROOSTER

The rooster is the tenth sign of the Chinese zodiac.

Years
1921, 1933, 1945, 1957,
1969, 1981, 1993, 2005

Element
metal

Hour
between 5 and 7 p.m.

Compass direction
between 247.5 and 277.5 degrees – west

Good luck sector
west

To energize good wealth luck in your good luck sector there are several symbolic things you can apply:

• Place images of the rooster in the sector of your house that falls between the degrees indicated above. To enhance its intrinsic energy display rooster images and sculptures that are made of ceramics or porcelain.

• Activate the sector with the metal element since this is the intrinsic element of your animal sign. Thus bells and wind chimes are fine. It will be bad luck for you if this sector (west) is afflicted with a toilet or a kitchen since this would cause your personalized sector to be badly affected.

• Rooster year people also benefit from sectors that correspond to the animal years of the snake and the ox. The direction of the snake is south-southeast and the ox is north-northeast.

Rooster year people are advised to observe the following ideas to improve their luck:

The years of the dragon (2000) are excellent periods that benefit from the wealth vase and the gem tree. Other excellent enhancers are the three-legged toad and water features with goldfish in the north.

In the years of the snake (2001) the good luck period continues. Display or wear good fortune coins and keep fish for the luck of abundance.

The years of the horse (2002) are difficult years for roosters when plans go awry and love life gets seriously afflicted. Place the Laughing Buddha in the east to help dissolve problems caused by the Five Yellow, and have a pair of mandarin ducks in your bedroom. Do not sit facing south.

The years of the sheep (2003) have very good mentor luck although money fortunes are mediocre. Energize the northwest with a six-rod wind chime and keep the Fuk Luk Sau three Star Gods in the dining room.

In the years of the monkey (2004) financial problems can be reduced with the presence of the dragon tortoises and fu dogs. Place crystal balls in the southwest for harmony of family life, a wind chime in the center of your home to counter the Five Yellow, and do not sit facing west-southwest.

In the years of the rooster (2005) fortunes revive. Energize the west with wind chimes (seven rods) and the north with a three-legged toad.

The years of the dog (2006) benefit from prosperity and wealth energizers. Place the God of Wealth in the right sector and create a wealth vase.

In the years of the boar (2007) energize the luck of the southwest by placing crystals and crystal balls there. Place *chi lins* in the house for protection against betrayal.

THE DOG

The dog is the eleventh sign of the Chinese zodiac.

Years
1922, 1934, 1946, 1958,
1970, 1982, 1994, 2006

Element
earth

Hour
between 7 and 9 p.m.

Compass direction
between 277.5 and 307.5 degrees – west-northwest

Good luck sector
west-northwest

To energize good wealth luck in your good luck sector there are several symbolic things you can apply:

• Place images of the dog in the sector of your house that falls between the degrees indicated above. To enhance its intrinsic energy, display dog images and sculptures made of ceramics or porcelain. This enhances the earth element.

• Activate the sector with other objects that suggest the earth element since this is the intrinsic element of your animal sign. It will be bad luck for you if a toilet or the kitchen is placed here (west-northwest) since this would seriously afflict your sector.

• Dog year people also benefit from sectors that correspond to the animal years of the tiger and the horse. The direction of the tiger is east-northeast and the direction of the horse is south. Dog year people are advised to do the following to improve their luck:

The years of the dragon (2000) are tiresome when things go wrong. Place fu dogs and tortoises for protection against loss of face and money. Dangerous adversaries require amulets for protection. Stay cool but hang wind chimes in the north to overcome the Five Yellow and do not sit facing the Grand Duke in the east-southeast.

In the years of the snake (2001) fortunes take a sharp upswing. Place metal objects in the northwest for mentor luck and use prosperity enhancers such as the three-legged toad and good luck coins.

The years of the horse (2002) are years of expansion and money luck. Magnify good fortune with the *chi lin* and the *ru yi*. Career luck is very obvious this year.

In the years of the sheep (2003) there are small setbacks but these can be nullified by placing wind chimes or bells in the southeast since this will exhaust the deadly Five Yellow. Place a bright chandelier in the south-southwest to energize.

The years of the monkey (2004) will be smooth. Maintain harmony by placing Yin Yang balls in the west-southwest.

In the years of the rooster (2005) there are emotional setbacks. Dissipate unhappiness with the Laughing Buddha in the living room and the Fuk Luk Sau in the dining room.

In the years of the dog (2006) place fu dogs in the dog's home direction (west-northwest) to ensure that disputes do not get out of hand.

The years of the boar (2007) are quiet periods that benefit from the presence in the house of the double happiness calligraphy as well as longevity symbols such as the peach, the crane, or the deer. These images can be on paintings or displayed as ceramics. Hang an eight-rod wind chime in the northeast to overcome the Five Yellow.

THE BOAR

The boar is the twelfth sign of the Chinese zodiac.

Years
1923, 1935, 1947, 1959,
1971, 1983, 1995, 2007

Element
water

Hour
between 9 and 11 p.m.

Compass direction
between 307.5 and 337.5 degrees – north-northwest

Good luck sector
north-northwest

To energize good wealth luck in your good luck sector there are several symbolic things you can apply:

• Place images of the boar in the sector of your house that falls between the degrees indicated above. To enhance its intrinsic energy, display boar images next to water. This enhances the water element of this animal sign.

• Activate the sector with water features such as aquariums and fishponds since water is the intrinsic element of your animal sign. It will be bad luck for you if a toilet or the kitchen is placed here (north-northwest) since this would seriously afflict your sector.

• Boar year people also benefit from sectors that correspond to the years of the sheep and the rabbit. The direction of the sheep is south-southwest and the direction of the rabbit is east.

Boar year people are advised to observe the following ideas to improve their luck:

The years of the dragon (2000) are very smooth and happy and are excellent for career and relationships. You will benefit from a horse image in the south. Place a six-rod wind chime in the northwest.

The years of the snake (2001) are not good because there will be some financial setbacks. Place a pair of fu dogs at your entrance door. Health problems will surface. Place the God of Longevity in your home. Hang wind chimes in the southwest to overcome the Five Yellow and do not sit directly facing the Grand Duke, which is in the south-southeast this year.

In the years of the horse (2002) fortunes will rebound. Place the three-legged toad in the living room for money-making opportunities and have the double happiness symbol nearby for romance luck.

The years of the sheep (2003) have good career luck. Install an aquarium in the north and keep nine goldfish to enhance chances of promotion.

In the years of the monkey (2004) place a pair of *chi lins* to protect you from being overwhelmed by financial problems. Also put a dragon tortoise in the north. Place wind chimes in the center of your home to protect from the Five Yellow.

In the years of the rooster (2005) you will need all the prosperity enhancers to boost your money luck. Also display a gem tree in your living room and try making a wealth vase.

The years of the dog (2006) are a quiet period when the best thing you can do is to invite in the three Star Gods if you have not already done so.

In the years of the boar (2007) there is good money luck. Place a water feature in the north and a six-rod wind chime in the northwest.

Afterword

My dear readers,

There is no more auspicious symbol than the precious Laughing Buddha since above all things he symbolizes the true happiness that comes from transforming other people's problems into happiness. I love the Laughing Buddhas that I have in my home because these images remind me of the motivation that must lie behind my books. I write about Feng Shui because I genuinely believe it is a wonderful science that must be shared. When used correctly, it has the power to transform problems into happiness and to create the circumstances for success luck as well as to manifest your many different aspirations.

LILLIAN TOO

To date I have written 42 books on the subject, which have been translated into 21 languages. I am a little overwhelmed at the great blossoming of worldwide interest in Feng Shui. Once again I thank all those masters and experts who have over the years helped me. In particular I thank again my si fu, Master Yap Cheng Hai, who is also my wonderful big brother. Indeed, we have been through some great adventures together and much of the formula Feng Shui I have learned has been due to his great kindness in sharing his knowledge with me. In many ways he has opened my eyes and my inquisitive mind to seek more knowledge through research and additional study.

This book on symbolic Feng Shui has been one result of my continuing study. I have really loved writing it and I hope you enjoy and benefit from it as much. Please join my growing network of readers by coming to my on-line Feng Shui magazine at www.wofs.com, short for www.worldoffengshui.com, where you can read more about this fascinating science.

THE LAUGHING BUDDHA SYMBOLIZES TRUE HAPPINESS. THIS PIECE IS PART OF THE AUTHOR'S PRIVATE COLLECTION.

Lillian Too

A Sampling of What Others Say

Lillian Too's Feng Shui website has been big news. Feng Shui is the Chinese art of geomancy – a cross between psychic energy and interior design – and Lillian Too can make a Swiss ski chalet seem as spiritual as Stonehenge ... in Asia she is a celebrity and her online consultations are burning up lots of Asian band-width.

WIRED, USA

Highly readable and with interesting anecdotes, Lillian Too's Feng Shui should interest everyone who seeks to understand the forces of Nature ... it is an invaluable addition to the growing literature on Eastern thinking and Lillian Too is to be congratulated for her timely contribution.

DR. TARCISIUS CHIN, CEO

... Too is a person who practices what she preaches.

NEW STRAITS TIMES

... to the readers of her bestselling books throughout Malaysia, Lillian Too has only just begun.

BUSINESS TIMES

Too's credentials are impeccable.

SARAWAK SUNDAY TRIBUNE

... she is not the sort of proponent of this ancient Chinese art who peddles her knowledge to companies ... what she does, and has done with considerable success, is write books about Feng Shui.

SMART INVESTOR

Too distills the essence of the practice and explains in simple terms how Feng Shui can improve anyone's life.

VOGUE MAGAZINE

... An interesting read – I found myself looking at my apartment in a totally different way.

THE OBSERVER, UK, ON FENG SHUI FUNDAMENTALS

... Donald Trump, Olivia Newton John and Boy George have all had their homes feng shui-ed by experts ... BUT Lillian Too's Feng Shui Kit contains all you need to do it yourself.

THE MIRROR, UK

Further Reading

OTHER LILLIAN TOO BOOKS

Basic Feng Shui, KONSEP BOOKS, 1997

Chinese Astrology for Romance and Relationships,
KONSEP BOOKS, 1996

The Complete Illustrated Guide to Feng Shui,
ELEMENT BOOKS, 1996

The Complete Illustrated Guide to Feng Shui for Gardens,
ELEMENT BOOKS, 1998

Creating Abundance with Feng Shui, RIDER, 1999

Easy to Use Feng Shui, COLLINS & BROWN, 1999

Feng Shui, KONSEP BOOKS, 1993

Feng Shui – 168 Tips for Success, COLLINS & BROWN, 1999

Feng Shui – 168 Tips for Love, COLLINS & BROWN, 2000

Feng Shui Essentials, RIDER, 1997

Feng Shui Fundamentals: Careers

   Feng Shui Fundamentals: Children

   Feng Shui Fundamentals: Education

   Feng Shui Fundamentals: Eight Easy Lessons

   Feng Shui Fundamentals: Fame

   Feng Shui Fundamentals: Health

   Feng Shui Fundamentals: Love

   Feng Shui Fundamentals: Networking

   Feng Shui Fundamentals: Wealth

ELEMENT BOOKS, 1997

Flying Star Feng Shui, KONSEP BOOKS, 1994

The Illustrated Encyclopedia of Feng Shui,
ELEMENT BOOKS, 1999

Inner Feng Shui, RIDER, 2000

Lillian Too's Feng Shui Kit, ELEMENT BOOKS, 1997

The Little Book of Feng Shui, ELEMENT BOOKS, 1998

The Little Book of Feng Shui at Work, ELEMENT BOOKS, 1999

Practical Applications of Feng Shui,
KONSEP BOOKS, 1994

Water Feng Shui for Wealth,
KONSEP BOOKS, 1995

LILLIAN TOO'S WEBSITES

You are invited to visit the world's first completely online Feng Shui magazine at:
http://www.worldoffengshui.com

Lillian Too's official author website where you can check out all of her Feng Shui books and browse through Lillian's photo album, read her press cuttings, enjoy her Feng Shui tips, and check out her program of talks and seminars:
http://www.lillian-too.com

Lillian Too's **Feng Shui Fine Jewelry** site where you can browse and shop online. OE Design created the beautiful pieces of real gold and diamond jewelry to Lillian's specifications. Every piece is designed to activate a specific type of luck (wealth, romance, career...) for the wearer using powerful symbolic Feng Shui enhancement.
http://www.lilliantoojewellery.com

Lillian Too, a graduate from the Harvard Business School in Boston, was the first woman in Asia to become the chief executive officer of a bank in 1982. Following a highly successful business career during the 1980s she retired from working life in the early 1990s and returned home to Malaysia to spend more time with her family and to devote her energy to writing. Her books on Feng Shui can be found in every corner of the globe; she has made the bestseller lists in the US, the UK, Germany, Holland, Norway, and South Africa; her work has been translated into more than fifteen languages.

Too lives in Kuala Lumpur, where she continues to write about and observe the principles of Feng Shui in her own home. She also contributes to numerous magazines and runs her own publishing company, all of which she does with marked success.